SALISBURY
IN 50

BUILDINGS

PAUL RABBITTS & LIZ GORDON

AMBERLEY

To David Rabbitts, born in Wiltshire, but raised in Yorkshire

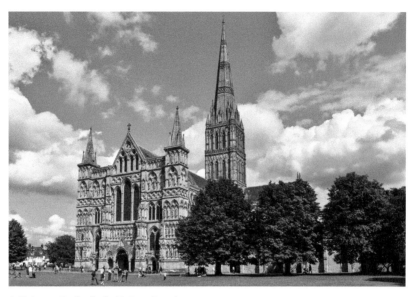

Salisbury Cathedral. (© Ian Scott)

First published 2021

Amberley Publishing, The Hill, Stroud
Gloucestershire GL5 4EP

www.amberley-books.com

British Library Cataloguing in Publication Data.
A catalogue record for this book is available from the British Library.

ISBN 978 1 4456 9932 5 (print)
ISBN 978 1 4456 9933 2 (ebook)

Typesetting by SJmagic DESIGN SERVICES, India.
Printed in Great Britain.

Contents

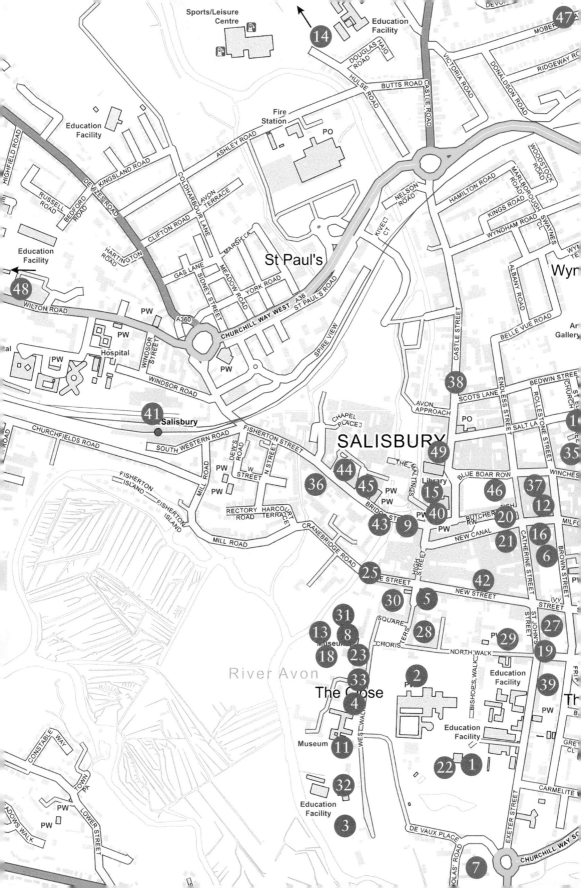

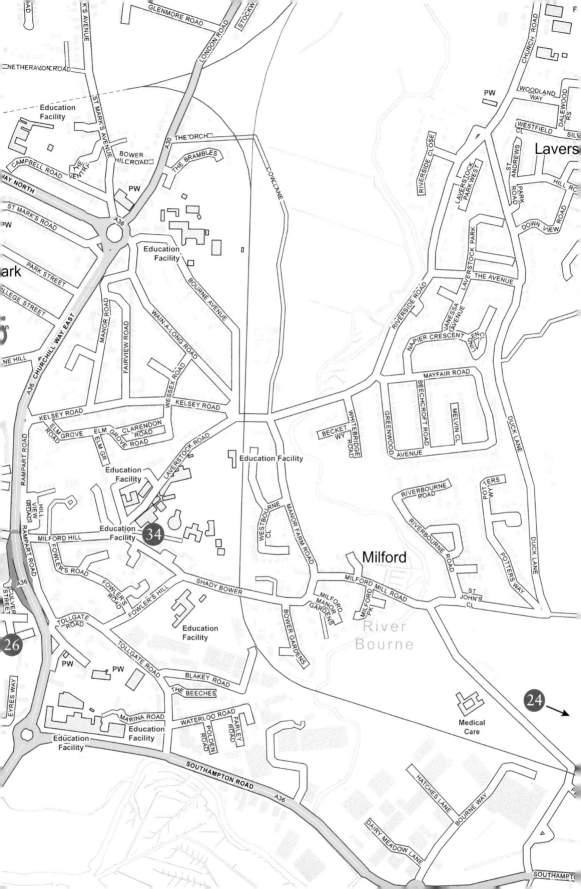

Key

Introduction

Salisbury, formerly New Sarum, is a city in the administrative and historic county of Wiltshire that is situated at the confluence of the rivers Avon and Wiley. It functioned historically as the principal town of Wiltshire and is the seat of an Anglican bishop.

The origins of Salisbury lie in Old Sarum, an early Iron Age fort 1.5 miles (2.5 km) north taken over by the Romans. Under the Saxons it became an important town and by the eleventh century it possessed a mint. The Normans built a castle on the mound, and Old Sarum became a bishopric in 1075. The stone structures of Old Sarum and the excavations of the post-Conquest castle date back to the twelfth and early thirteenth centuries, and are likely to have replaced earlier wooden buildings.

The present cathedral was founded in the neighbouring valley, the site of which became modern Salisbury in 1220, and a new city quickly developed around it. The Black and Grey Friaries were both established in the thirteenth century. An earthen rampart was built around the city in 1310, with gates added soon afterwards. The cloth and wool trades flourished in the Middle Ages, and the making of cutlery also became prominent.

Today the city centre remains much as it was in medieval times, laid out in a gridiron fashion. The cathedral and a large number of timber-framed buildings survive. Salisbury today is a thriving tourist and market centre. Its principal occupations are cattle and poultry marketing, engineering, brewing, leatherwork and printing.

The architecture of Salisbury has ensured that the city is now regarded as one of the world's finest medieval cities. It thankfully retains most of its original layout with an exceptionally fine collection of historic buildings dating from the medieval period, and each one is dominated by the tallest spire in England – 123 metres. So magnificent are these buildings that it was one of the few cities that, in 1980, was surveyed in detail by the Royal Commission on Historic Monuments. This included over 700 buildings. The delights of Salisbury's streetscapes rely on the many architecturally rich buildings and there are few cities that have such a harmonious collection – ranging from a rich mix of timber-framing, flint, ashlar, brick, tile hanging and slate.

Salisbury has been rigidly divided into two parts: the religious enclave around the cathedral and the secular world outside of it. Since the early fourteenth century

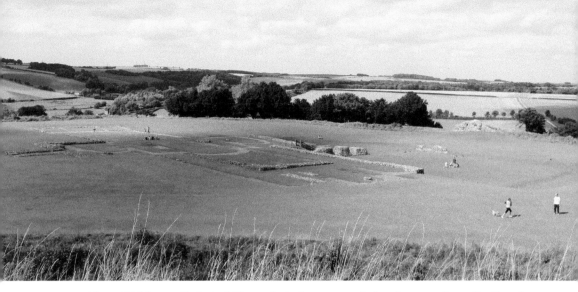

Above: Old Sarum Cathedral. The cathedral was created after the 1075 Council of London decreed that the episcopal see should be moved from Sherborne to Old Sarum. The bishop at the time was Herman, but the major work was completed under his successor, Osmund (1078–99), who shaped the character and constitution of Old Sarum Cathedral.

The first small cathedral was magnificently extended eastwards by Bishop Roger (1102–39). At his death in 1139, plans to rebuild the nave were abandoned and it was left to Bishop Jocelyn (1142–84) to furnish and fit out the enlarged cathedral, as well as add a new west front. In addition to the cathedral, a precinct for the cathedral canons and bishop's palace had been created to the north under Osmund and Roger, to which a cloister was added, in all likelihood under Jocelyn.

Below: Old Sarum Castle. It is William the Conqueror's recognition of Old Sarum's potential shortly after the Conquest that has left the greatest mark on Old Sarum. A motte was thrown up in the centre of the hill fort, creating an inner set of fortifications, with a huge outer bailey wrapped around this inner core. All early buildings in the castle would have been of timber, and the oldest surviving stone structure, the keep, was probably built early in the reign of Henry I (1100–35). In around 1130, however, the castle was made over to Roger, Bishop of Sarum and regent for Henry I during the king's absences in Normandy.

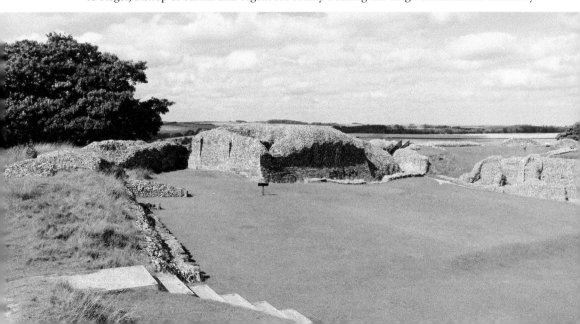

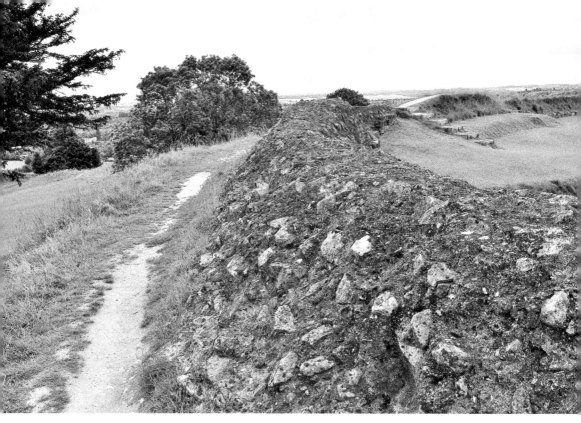

The old outer wall at Old Sarum.

that division has been enforced by the defensive Close wall. Today, Cathedral Close is one of the most prestigious addresses in England, described by Defoe in the early eighteenth century as 'the Circle of Ground wall'd in adjacent to the Cathedral…[was]…like another City'.

Writing this book was therefore a challenge from the outset. With such a plethora of magnificent buildings to choose from, attempting to narrow down to a list of fifty was always going to be difficult. There were clear and obvious ones to include, and many will say that others have been missed off. However, we have attempted to show the diversity of buildings in Salisbury, from use of materials, building use and purpose, period and style to, where possible, the introduction of more modern architecture.

Salisbury's buildings did occasionally throw up the odd surprise. The former chapel of St John is one such building and appears quite insignificant, yet it is one of the very few remaining bridge chapels to survive in England. Behind the bow and beneath the render is the virtually intact chapel of St John, built on the island between the two sections of the Ayleswade Bridge across the River Avon. It more than likely dates from 1340. Now a house, it measures 10 metres long by 8 metres wide – this was a wonderful discovery.

The incredible history of Salisbury is covered elsewhere (see Bibliography) but it is hoped that the buildings chosen and described in this book are all worthy of inclusion.

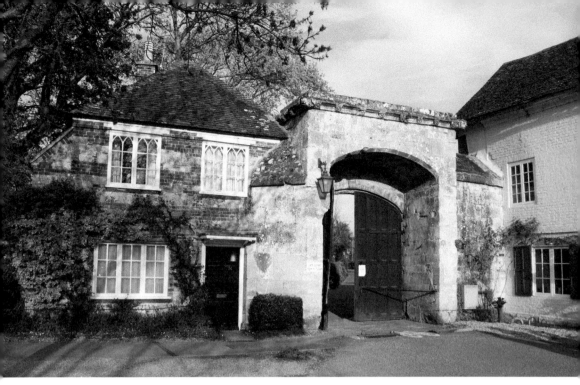

Above: Harnham Gate, or South Gate, stands at one end of Harnham Bridge near Cathedral Close. This arched stone entry is an English Heritage listed building. Believed to have been built in the thirteenth century, it is the least grand and the smallest of the four gates to the Close.

Below: St Anne's Gate was probably begun in around 1327 but was extended shortly afterwards on at least two occasions and a chapel added above it. This room was later incorporated into Malmesbury House next door and is where Handel once played. The chapel windows are Victorian replacements, dated 1852. (© Howard Somerville)

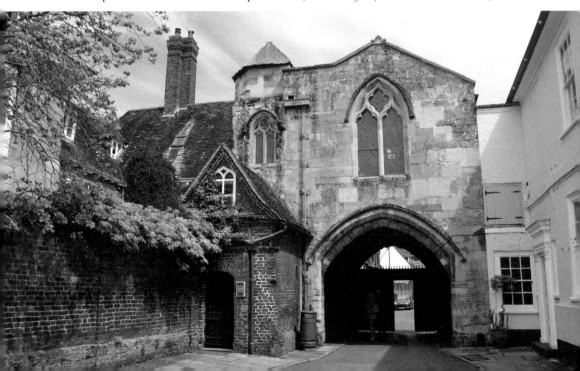

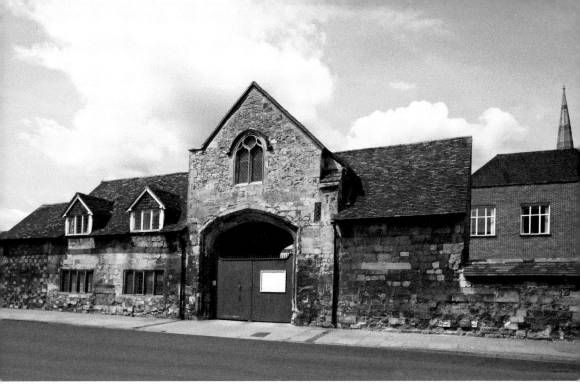

Above: Bishop's Gate. The last gate to be built in the Close defences was added when Bishop Erghum began fortifying the Bishop's Palace after 1377, and this gate became the main entrance to it.

Right: North Gate or High Street Gate to Cathedral Close still acts as a barrier between the city and the cathedral. This gate was built soon after the licence to fortify Cathedral Close was granted in 1327 and it is comparatively unaltered. The front facing the High Street was rebuilt a century or so later. The royal arms over the gateway were probably added to mark the Restoration of 1660.

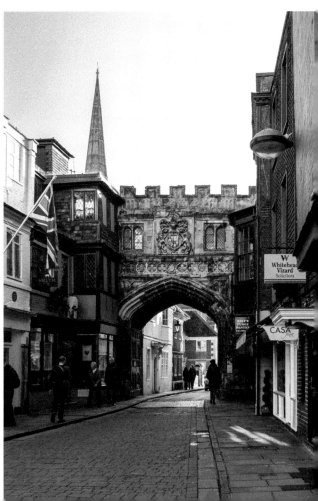

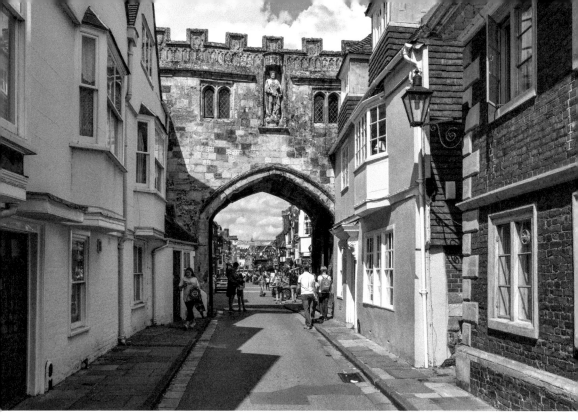

Above: North Gate looking towards the High Street. (© Ian Scott)

Below: Chapel of St John.

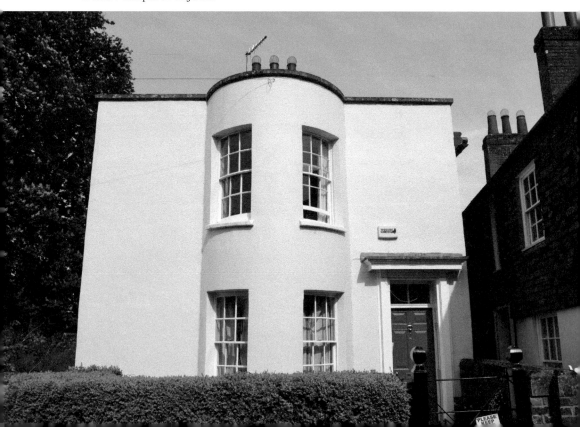

The 50 Buildings

1. Salisbury Cathedral School

One of the least known yet most important buildings in Salisbury is the former Bishop's Palace. First built when the city was established in the 1220s, it was home to successive bishops for over 700 years until becoming the Cathedral School in 1946.

The Bishop's Palace grew from his first residence called 'New Place', already established by 1219. The first simple building was added to and altered by succeeding bishops until it gained its present form of a series of irregular buildings running from east to west, the most striking feature being a late fifteenth- or early sixteenth-century tower with its decorated turret. A fifteenth-century bedchamber was converted into a chapel in the mid-sixteenth century. Part of the original building survives in the vaulted undercroft known as Bishop Poore's Hall. This was restored by Bishop Wordsworth in 1889. During the period of the Commonwealth, the palace was let out by the corporation in tenements, one of which was kept as an inn by a Dutch tailor. After these depredations of this period, the house was completely restored by Bishop Seth Ward. The gardens were laid out and a lake formed in the mid-nineteenth century, at which time the stables and an entrance lodge were added. In 1947, the Church Commissioners exchanged the

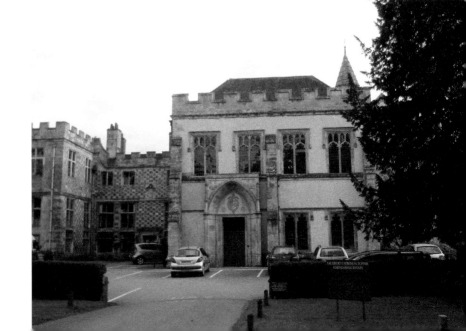

Salisbury Cathedral School, one of the oldest buildings in Salisbury.

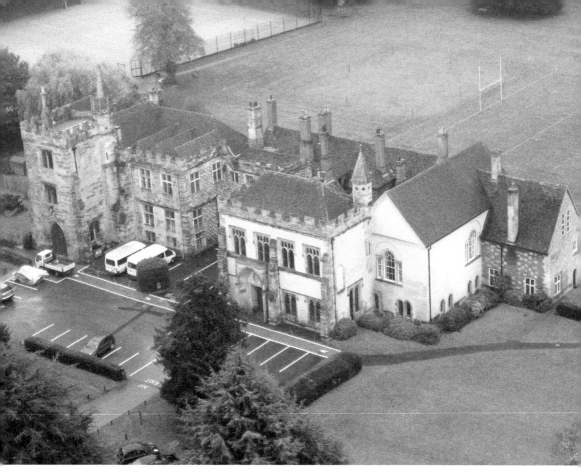

Founded in 1091, the school is now located in the former Bishop's Palace.

palace with the dean and chapter for Mompesson House. The palace then became the premises of the Cathedral School, and the bishop moved his residence for a time to Mompesson House.

One of the oldest educational establishments in the world, Salisbury Cathedral School was founded in 1091 by St Osmund, nephew of William the Conqueror and Bishop of Salisbury, to educate the choristers of his cathedral at Old Sarum, a mile away from the present site.

After 150 years at Old Sarum, the choristers' school moved to Salisbury, following the building of the new cathedral and, in 1947, the school finally came to its present home, based in the twelfth-century buildings and grounds of the former Bishop's Palace. Today the choristers of Salisbury Cathedral are educated at the school.

2. Salisbury Cathedral

The Grade I listed Salisbury Cathedral (formally known as the Cathedral Church of the Blessed Virgin Mary) is one of the leading examples of Early English architecture. The main body of the cathedral was completed in only thirty-eight years, from 1220 to 1258. The cathedral is the mother church of the diocese of Salisbury and seat of the bishop of Salisbury.

As a response to deteriorating relations between the clergy and the military at Old Sarum Cathedral, the decision was taken to resite the cathedral and the bishopric was moved to Salisbury. The move occurred during the tenure of Bishop Richard Poore, a wealthy man who donated the land on which it was built. The new cathedral was paid for by donations, principally from the canons and vicars of south-east England who were asked to contribute a fixed annual sum until it was completed.

The foundation stone was laid on 28 April 1220. Much of the freestone for the cathedral came from nearby Teffont Evias quarries. As a result of the high-water table in the new location, the cathedral was built on only 4 feet of foundations, and by 1258 the nave, transepts and choir were complete. The only major sections built later were the cloisters in 1240, the chapter house in 1263, and tower and spire, which at 404 feet dominated the skyline from 1320. Because most of the cathedral was built in only thirty-eight years, it has a single consistent architectural style – Early English Gothic. The design of this magnificent cathedral is attributed to two people: Elias of Dereham, canon of the cathedral, and Nicholas of Ely, a master mason.

Although the spire is the cathedral's most impressive feature, it has proved to be troublesome. Together with the tower it added 6,397 tons to the weight of the building. Without the addition of buttresses, bracing arches and anchor irons over

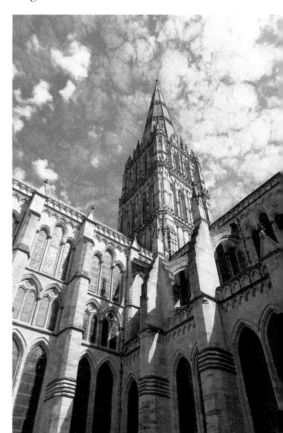

Salisbury Cathedral and its impressive spire.
(© Glen Joe Davies)

the succeeding centuries, it would have suffered the fate of spires on later great ecclesiastical buildings (such as Malmesbury Abbey) and fallen down; instead, Salisbury remains the tallest church spire in the UK. The large supporting pillars at the corners of the spire are seen to bend inwards under the stress. The addition of reinforcing tie beams above the crossing, designed by Sir Christopher Wren in 1668, arrested further deformation. The beams were hidden by a false ceiling, installed below the lantern stage of the tower.

Significant changes to the cathedral were made by the architect James Wyatt in 1790, including replacement of the original rood screen and demolition of a bell tower, which stood around 320 feet north-west of the main building. Salisbury is one of only three English cathedrals to lack a ring of bells; the others are Norwich Cathedral and Ely Cathedral. However, it does strike the time every 15 minutes with bells. In total, 70,000 tons of stone, 3,000 tons of timber and 450 tons of lead were used in the construction of the cathedral.

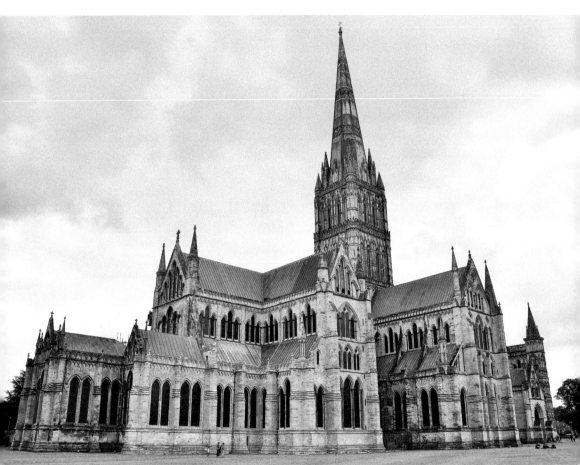

The cathedral is attributed to Elias of Dereham, canon of the cathedral, and Nicholas of Ely, a master mason. (© Ben Abel)

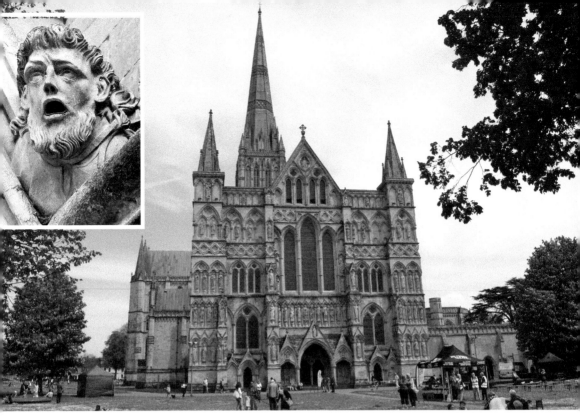

Above: The magnificence and Early English Gothic architectural style of Salisbury Cathedral. (© Ben Abel)

Inset: Stone detail from the cathedral.

Below: The cloisters of the cathedral, added in 1240. (© Ben Abel)

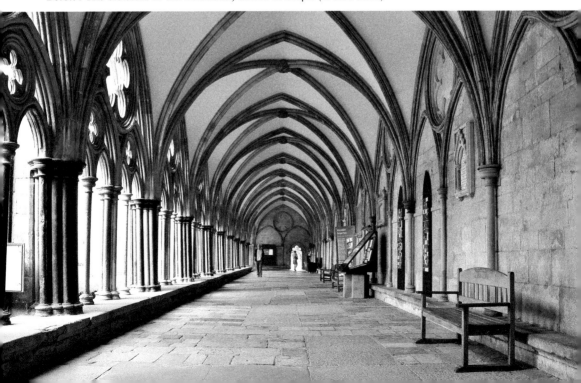

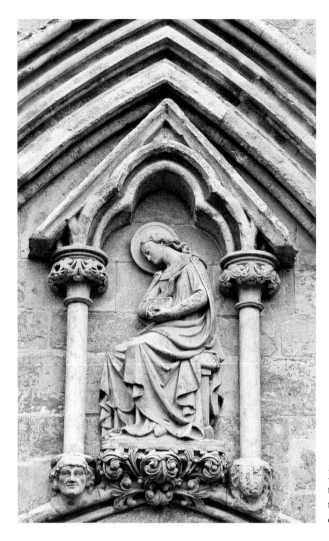

Much of the stone for the cathedral came from the nearby Teffont Evias quarries. (© Ben Abel)

3. Leaden Hall

Cathedral Close is one of the most beautiful in Britain, as well as being one of the most desirable places to live. The man whose overall concept and plan it was to build the cathedral was Elias of Dereham. During the erection of the cathedral it is likely he built himself the house facing it, although by 1232 the house was in existence.

At the time it was known as Aula Plumbea (Leaden Hall) because of the costly lead roof. Today, little of this roof remains, and the house itself is mostly a 1717 façade on the original house. At one side some of the original wall and windows can be seen, and in the garden there stood a small stone cross from the early chapel.

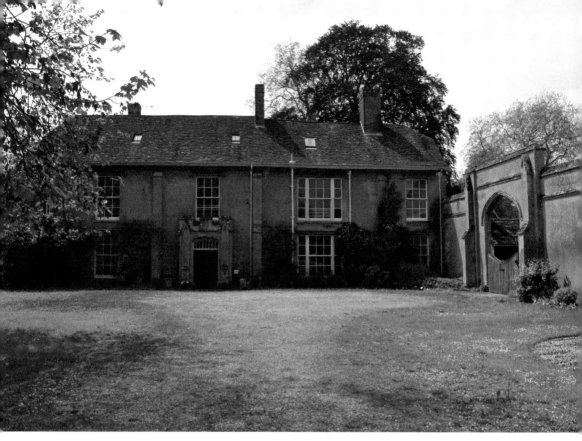

Leaden Hall, the home for many important residents over several centuries.

Many tenants have lived in Leaden Hall, including several chancellors of the cathedral and Henry Chicheley, who in 1414 became Archbishop of Canterbury. He is the archbishop mentioned by Shakespeare in Henry V.

John Constable, possibly the most famous of English landscape painters, lived and painted in Leaden Hall as a guest of his great friend Bishop Fisher. His painting of the cathedral from the house is now in the National Gallery. *Harnham Mill* is another painting from Leaden Hall, and also *The White Horse*, which is now part of the Frick Collection in New York.

In 1951, when a south wall was replastered, the original lath and plaster wall was found and a small Norman arch revealed, but this had to be recovered for modern use. Leaden Hall remained a canonical residence until 1947 and, in 1948, it became a private preparatory school.

4. North Canonry, West Walk

A flint and Chilmark stone house of thirteenth century origin, the North Canonry was largely rebuilt in the sixteenth and seventeenth centuries. It was also restored by Sir Giles Gilbert Scott in the nineteenth century. It is not as set back as other nearby houses and has a picturesque, unsymmetrical front, but is a fine building.

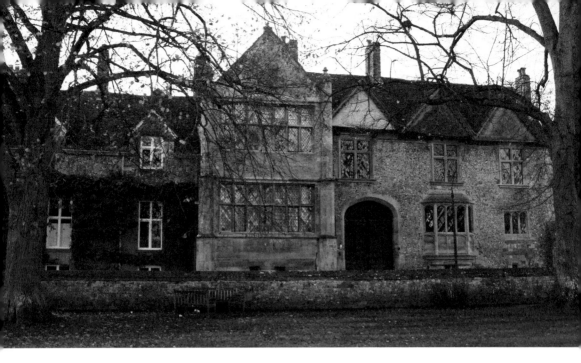

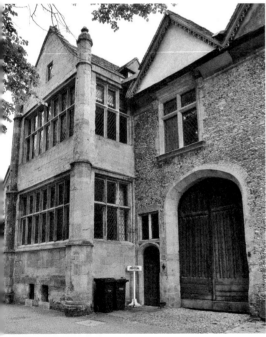

Above: North Canonry on West Walk.

Left: North Canonry on West Walk. (© Ben Abel)

5. Mitre House

The Mitre House, which is reputed to be the first house to have been built in the city of Salisbury, has a long association with the cathedral. Tradition has it that Bishop Richard Poore had a temporary lodging here to oversee the building of the

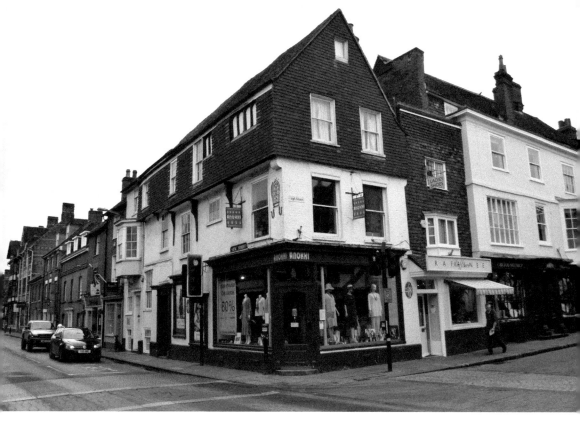

Mitre House, once an inn. (© Matt Brown)

church. By 1620, it was an inn, known initially as the Holy Lamb, and later as the Sun and Lamb. By ancient custom, the bishops of Salisbury use Mitre House as a robing place before their enthronement – hence its present name.

6. Red Lion Hotel

Originally called the White Bear Inn, this building was constructed to house the draughtsman working on the new cathedral when the churchmen of the time fell out with the military garrison on the hilltop castle at Old Sarum. When the basic construction was finished in the late thirteenth century the White Bear continued to house visitors to the cathedral, and subsequently the 'New City' of Salisbury. It is therefore possible that the hotel is the longest running purpose-built hotel in the country.

The earliest part of the building is the south wing, with many beams and numerous examples of wattle and daub that have since been exposed. The open gallery of the upper storey that once looked down upon the courtyard was sealed during the nineteenth century. Outside the hotel ran one of the main watercourses for which Salisbury was famous. It was here that the 'cage and ducking stool' was sited. It was a method of punishment for scalds, nagging women and short-changing shopkeepers, who were ducked in what was no more than a deep, smelly open sewer, no doubt to the delight of onlookers who then returned to the inn for refreshment.

In the early 1700s the name was changed to the Red Lion and Cross Keys. This name remained in use until 30 January 1769 when the sign was altered to the 'Red Lion' only by Daniel Safe, who bought the property following Ralph Musselwhite in 1766. When Daniel Pearce Safe, the postmaster of Salisbury, took over the ownership of the Red Lion, he immediately transferred the Salisbury post office to the hotel building. As a result, the Red Lion became the main entrance for all mail coaches arriving in and leaving Salisbury.

The Red Lion Hotel was extremely important to commercial travellers journeying along the route between London and Exeter during the eighteenth, nineteenth and twentieth centuries. The hotel was used as the headquarters and clubhouse of the Salisbury Rugby Club after it was formed there in 1881. The Red Lion Hotel has also been used in the past by the military. In the late 1770s, troops were quartered upon it, much to the resentment of the hotel's owner. The troop's rowdy and unruly behaviour cost him money and deterred other travellers from staying. During the First World War, Australian troops staying at nearby Codford used the hotel; however, their equally unruly behaviour resulted in the hotel losing a large double bed, which the Australians took home as a souvenir when they left Salisbury in 1918.

More importantly to the local community, the hotel offered farmers from rural villages an ideal place to stay while visiting Salisbury cattle market. It was also much used by traders visiting the nearby market, which is still held on Tuesdays and Saturdays to this day in the Market Square.

The Red Lion Hotel has played an important role in the history of Salisbury.

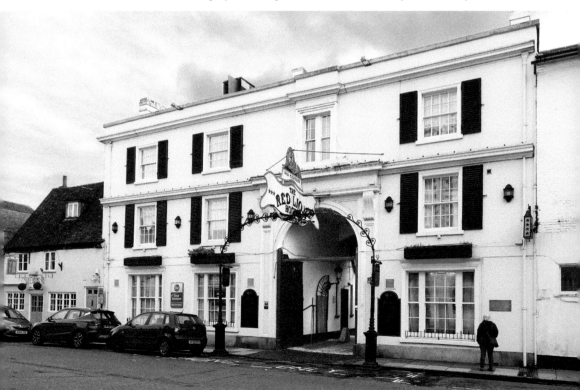

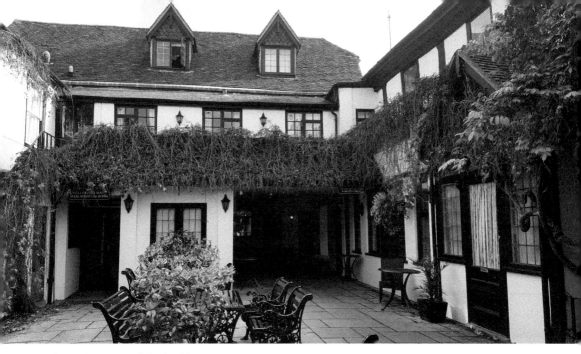

The earliest part of the building.

The origin of St Nicholas Hospital is unknown, but a charter of Richard Aucher, dated 1215, refers to the hospital as being already substantially established. Further gifts from Ela, Countess of Salisbury, wife of William Longspee, Earl of Salisbury, and Bishop Richard Poore are dated 1227. Substantial changes were made by Bishop Robert Bingham after 1229, sufficient for him to claim the role of founder. It is possible, for instance, that he rebuilt the hospital itself (royal grants of timber were made for the roof in 1231 and 1235), as most of the surviving medieval buildings date from the period of his episcopate. He also connected the hospital to his new two-part stone bridge (on which stood the chapel of St John, later a chantry) over the River Avon, which proved of enormous importance to the growing, newly resited city of Salisbury; travellers may have enriched St Nicholas's with gifts and alms.

Bingham ensured that a warden was appointed for the hospital in 1244 and declared that the purpose of the hospital was to receive, help and maintain the poor of Christ, the weak and the sick (*debilies et infirmi*). The hospital was apparently built in the form of a church, with a double hall divided down the centre by an arcade of seven arches, and opening into two chapels at the east end. The chapels remain, but the north aisle has gone. It is probable that the double hall served as a sick ward with the central aisle dividing the sexes, although another possibility is that one aisle may have been for the parochial use of the hospital's tenants. An earlier hospital, noted in 1227 as lying north of the new building, may be incorporated in the complex known as the North Building (restored 1860).

By 1478, statutes of Bishop Beauchamp reveal that St Nicholas Hospital had become – like many small, and often increasingly impoverished, hospitals – an almshouse, with a dozen brethren and sisters. Changes in the late Middle Ages are poorly documented, although in the early eighteenth century it was claimed changes were made around 1498, and this may be when the north aisle of the hall was removed. The south aisle was converted into six rooms for the inmates, with rooms for the master and chaplain above, while the north chapel became a common hall. Other rooms may have lain in a north block.

The hospital escaped dissolution under Edward VI, and was refounded in 1610 with the bishop holding the right to appoint the warden. It continues as an almshouse to the present day. The complex was sensitively restored by widely respected Victorian architect William Butterfield and others between *c.* 1850 and 1884.

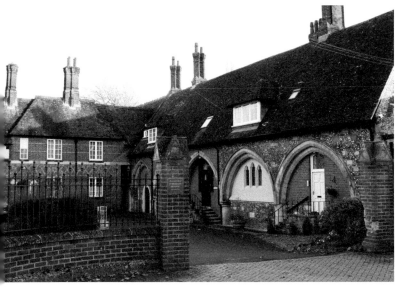

St Nicholas Hospital, which dates back to the thirteenth century.

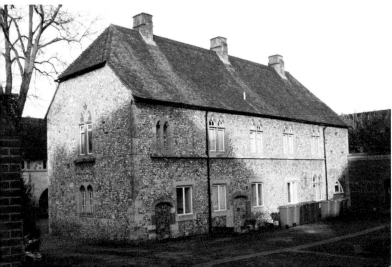

St Nicholas Hospital. The College of St Nicholas de Vaux, founded by Bishop Bridport in 1261 for twenty 'poor, needy, honourable and teachable scholars'. Students came from Oxford to form a thriving university here in the thirteenth and fourteenth centuries. Later it became an almshouse.

8. The King's House

One of the finest buildings in Salisbury is known as The King's House. It is now the home of the Salisbury and South West Wilts Museum, and home to the Pitt-Rivers collection.

Dating back to the thirteenth century, the house was referred to as the 'Court of the Abbott of Sherborne'. The abbot of Sherborne Abbey used this house as his prebendal residence in Salisbury prior to 1539, when Sherborne Abbey was decommissioned during the dissolution of the monasteries. During this period the house was known as Sherborne Palace. The administration of estates of religious houses seized in the Reformation was carried out by the Augmentation Court. Both this office and the dean and chapter of Salisbury Cathedral laid claim to the property; after much court wrangling the dean and chapter succeeded and still hold the freehold today.

The original house was considerably restructured in the fifteenth century and replaced with part of the present building. The fifteenth-century construction can be seen as the central frontage with three gables, and a porch that is thought to date to the thirteenth century. The building at that time would have had a great hall open to the roof, a parlour with a chamber above, service rooms and a kitchen. The original facing was decorated with flint rubble and herringbone tile courses. The original windows were of Ham Hill stone and traces of these are still visible on the frontage. The porch vaulting is also of Ham Hill stone, which is rare in buildings in Salisbury but common in Sherborne, which implies that the work was carried out during the Sherborne Abbey's tenancy.

In the sixteenth century the dean and chapter of Salisbury Cathedral let the house to a number of secular tenants. Around that period the north end of the house was extended with a large brick cross-wing, out of proportion to the original house. This work was carried out under the direction of the tenants, Thomas and Eleanor Sadler – Thomas was registrar to the bishops of Sarum. It is quite probable that it was in these rooms that James I and his wife, Anne of Denmark, were entertained when they visited in 1610 and 1613 – hence its name The King's House.

In the eighteenth century the tenancy was held by the Beach family, who sublet the property in smaller units. One of the tenants during this time was Lieutenant General Henry Shrapnel, inventor of the fragmenting artillery shell. Shrapnel is recorded as living at the house in 1785, which coincides closely with the time that he developed the shell.

In 1803, the house reverted to single occupancy for a short period, during which the tenancy was held by Sir John Slade from 1808 to 1852, although he ceased living there from 1829. Slade made a number of alterations to the building. In 1837, the house was sub-divided again and occupied by a Mr Henry Brodribb, a solicitor, and Miss Margaret Bazley (or Bazeley), headmistress of the Godolphin School, which was then housed in nearby Arundells. In 1837, the Godolphin

School moved into the King's House and was transferred in 1848 when an outbreak of cholera in the city forced its evacuation to premises on Milford Hill in another part of Salisbury.

From its vacancy by the Godolphin School, the King's House was used to accommodate the Diocesan Training College for Schoolmistresses. It was here at the Diocesan Training College that Thomas Hardy's sisters Kate and Mary were trained, possibly inspiring the attendance and escape from the Melchester (Salisbury) college of Sue Bridehead in *Jude the Obscure* wherein the college is described.

In 1966, the college became the College of Sarum St Michael, which closed in 1978, and a 125-year tenancy was taken up by Salisbury Museum, which moved into the building and opened its doors to the public in 1981.

In 1922, a wealthy American cosmetics manufacturer, Carl Weeks, and his wife, Edith, were impressed with the King's House and instructed their architects, William Whitney Rasmussen, Byron Boyd and Herbert Moore, to construct a similar family house in Des Moines, Iowa. The architects visited Salisbury, took details and arranged the purchase of authentic fittings locally, including stairs, fireplaces, panelling, flooring and other materials; many items were taken from No. 91 Crane Street, Salisbury. The project cost $1,500,000 for the building and $1,500,000 for furnishings, and took five years to complete. Now called Salisbury House, the Des Moines house is operated as a museum.

The King's House, now home to the Pitt-Rivers collection.

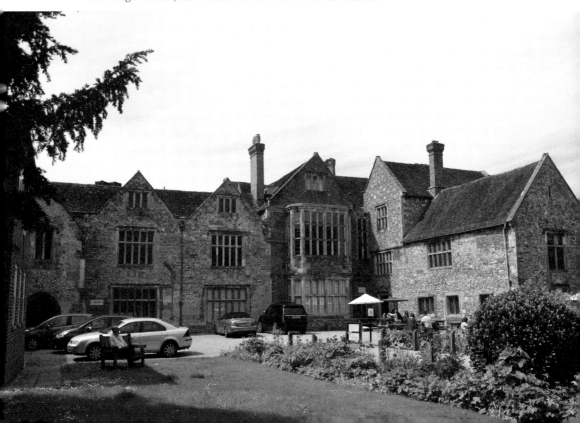

9. St Thomas' Church

Standing in the centre of the city, most of St Thomas' Church dates back to the fifteenth century and was originally a wooden structure built for those working on the 'new' cathedral. It is particularly renowned for the Doom painting of the Last Judgement that adorns the chancel arch – one of the largest and most complete in the UK. It was painted over in 1593 with the arms of Elizabeth I, then uncovered and restored in 1881. Further deterioration over time meant that further restoration was required and a fundraising campaign called Quest 2020 meant that in 2019 the stunning artwork was restored to its former glory. Remnants of other wall paintings from the fifteenth century are visible in the south chancel aisle.

There is mention of St Thomas in 1238, and the parish existed by 1246 in an area of the city where people first settled. The core of the current building is thought to have been built during the first half of the thirteenth century with a chapel built against it in the second half. The Godmanstone chantry was built on the northern side in the fourteenth century and the bell tower, built separate from the church, between 1400 and 1404 before becoming incorporated into the church in the late fifteenth century.

St Thomas' Church. (© Joe Katrencik)

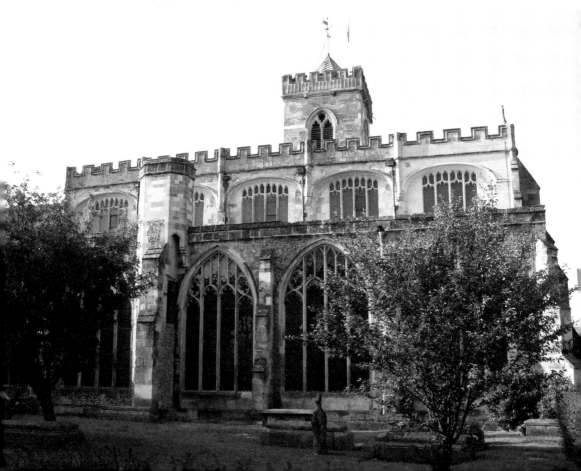

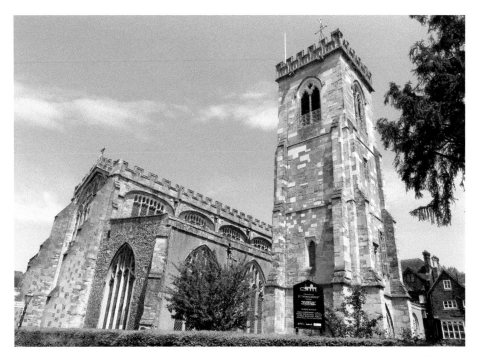

Like many historic churches, additions are often made; in this case it was the bell tower, built separate from the church between 1400 and 1404 before becoming incorporated into the church in the late fifteenth century.

Among the many alterations throughout its life, a rather unusual one affected the churchyard, which had become so high with burials that in 1719 the churchwardens were ordered to lower the soil level by 6 inches every year as it was considered a 'disgrace and a scandal'. The site closed for burials in 1854.

10. St Edmund's Church

St Edmund's Church, now Salisbury Arts Centre, has had a most fascinating history. In 1613, the church, which was founded in 1270 as a collegiate church with a provost and a college of around twelve canons, was bought by the parishioners. They found the upkeep of the building a great burden and it gradually fell into disrepair.

In 1407, the church had been almost completely rebuilt with a very imposing nave of 78 feet, a choir of equal length, transepts and a central tower and steeple. At the dissolution of the monasteries, the church, which also served as a parish church, and the college were seized by Henry VIII for the Crown and the canons dispersed. It passed into the hands of William St Barbe who, although a layman, became its first rector.

By 1613, the steeple had long since been removed. On Sunday 26 June the tower was in such a dangerous state that it swayed when the bells were rung. The next day, fortunately when no one was near the church, the tower collapsed and the nave was demolished. The fact that the tower was rebuilt almost immediately is remarkable as it was one of the few pieces of church building done during the commonwealth period.

On the wall of the tower is an ingenious chronogram: 'praIse hIM o yee ChILDren'. The date of the collapse is given by adding together those letters that could be used as Roman numerals. Many changes took place in the subsequent years, including those carried out by Sir George Gilbert Scott. There was at one time a three-decker pulpit and numerous pews, one of which even had its own fireplace.

During Scott's restoration between 1865 and 1867, the chancel was rebuilt with sacristy on the north and chapel on the south, with the former east walls of the fifteenth-century aisles taken down and re-erected to form the east end of the new extension. Flanking the east windows in both north and south chapel walls are the remains of two tiers of niches with vaulted canopies, which, until the Reformation, would have held statues of saints with lighted candles before them. On each side of the chancel is a two-arched arcade with octagonal piers and a

St Edmund's Church, now an arts centre. (© Ben Abel)

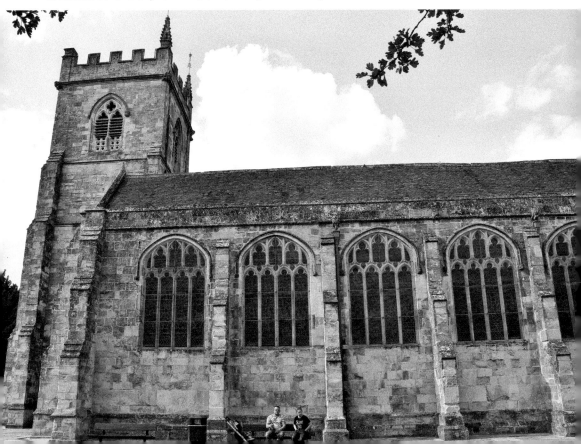

timber roof on shield corbels – all by Scott. The chancel arch and nave arcades are essentially medieval, though much restored.

The church was eventually adapted for use as an arts centre between 2003 and 2005.

11. Arundells

Arundells is one of the finest houses in the Cathedral Close, bringing together six distinct architectural styles. The house was originally a medieval canonry, with the first recorded occupant being Henry of Blunston, Archdeacon of Dorset, who lived here from 1291 until his death in 1316. Leonard Bilson, another canon, lived here until he was pilloried and imprisoned for acts of sorcery and magic in 1571.

A lease of the property was taken by Sir Richard Mompesson in 1609. He undertook major restoration works and the lease was transferred through his wife to her family, in whose occupation it remained until the end of the century.

John Wyndham became the tenant in 1718 and much of the rebuilding work that he undertook resulted in the house that exists today.

Arundells, one of the most well-known buildings in Salisbury and the former home of Sir Edward Heath, former prime minister.

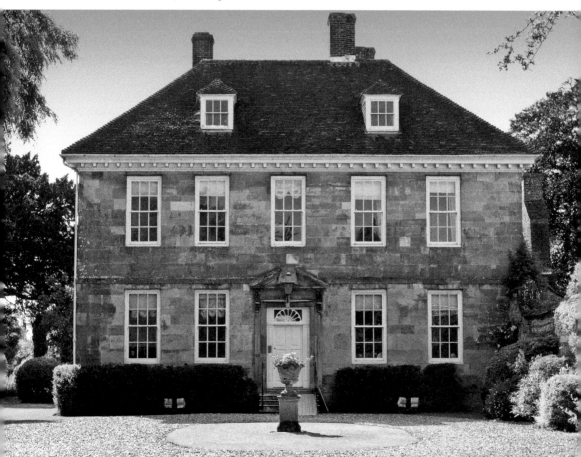

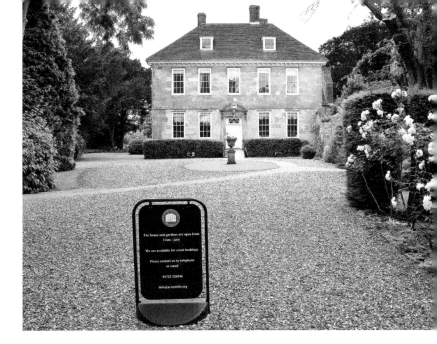

Arundells.
(© Ben Abel)

The name 'Arundells' comes from James Everard Arundel, son of the 6th Lord Arundel, who had married John Wyndham's daughter, Ann. The Arundels were a distinguished Roman Catholic family and Jesuit priests were sometimes secreted in the attic.

Arundells hosted the Godolphin Girls School (and later boarding school for boys) between 1839 and 1844. During the Second World War the house was used by the Red Cross as a centre for their library service and as a wool depot. The property fell into disrepair and demolition was considered following a long period of neglect. Extensive refurbishment works were undertaken by Mr and Mrs Robert Hawkings in 1964.

With paintings by Churchill and Sargent, Chinese ceramics from Chairman Mao, David Lloyd George's writing desk and memorabilia from Nixon and Castro, Arundells is also the former home of Sir Edward Heath KG MBE, prime minister (1970–74) and statesman. Today the house is one of Salisbury's most enchanting destinations. Sir Edward bequeathed Arundells to the charitable foundation set up in his name following his death in 2005. He very much wanted as many people as possible to 'share the beauty of Arundells' and to enjoy his diverse and very personal collection of artwork, photographs, sailing memorabilia and political cartoons.

The Friends of Arundells was founded in 2010 by a few committed people who, like many in the country, did not wish for Arundells and its valuable contents to be sold and lost forever.

12. William Russel's House and John a' Ports House, Nos 8 and 9 Queen Street

Often referred to as John a' Port's House, the house at No. 9 Queen Street, of three storeys with timber-framed walls and a tiled roof, dates mainly from the early fourteenth century and is a remarkably well-preserved building. In 1306,

Roger Hupewell, the holder of the land now occupied by Nos 9 and 10, sold a piece of ground to merchant William Russel with permission for Russel to build a wooden house beside that which already stood on the site of No. 10. Being opposite the Guildhall and Wool Market, it was often owned by wool merchants; these included Henry Russel (before 1354), Henry Fleming (1354–60), Thomas Hyndon (1363–98) and members of the Harding family (1398–1459). In 1435, Thomas Harding, draper of London, let the house to Richard and Alice Walker. The Walkers lived there until 1459 when the house was given to the cathedral by William Harding, clerk of the cathedral works. In 1649, the house comprised a shop, a kitchen, a buttery, a hall above stairs, four chambers, a garret, a courtyard and a stable.

Apart from the roof and the west front, both rebuilt between 1780 and 1790, William Russel's house of 1306–14 survives virtually intact. It is likely to be the oldest timber-framed house in Salisbury. It has had a number of more recent uses including Watson's China Shop, which was a local family firm established in 1834 and was present until 2008.

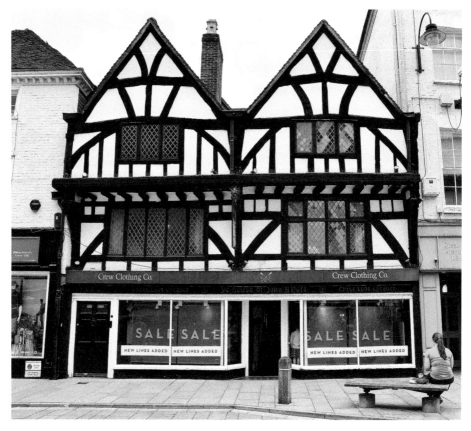

These twinned timber-framed buildings are often considered the oldest timber-framed buildings in Salisbury. (© Ben Abel)

13. Hemingsby House

This former canonry was named after Alexander de Hemingsby, who bequeathed it to the dean and chapter on his death in 1316. His name has also been applied to the earliest consecutive records of the chapter from 1329 until his death in 1334.

In the fifteenth century three canons of note – Upton, Fideon and Powell – occupied the dwelling. The first, Nicholas Upton, was the leading authority in his day on heraldry in England. As secretary to Thomas Montacute, Earl of Salisbury, he was at his side when the earl was killed in the unsuccessful defence of Orleans against Joan of Arc in 1428. He became precentor in 1446. Three years later, on the evening of the 3 June, he heard that a riot was taking place at the George Inn in the High Street. Together with Canon Walter Bayle, he collected the reserved host from the cathedral and carried it in procession to the High Street, at which the riot came to an abrupt end.

The focus of the trouble was the presence of Lord Moleyns, who gratefully accepted Nicholas Upton's offer of sanctuary in Cathedral Close. In 1456, Upton took a bag of gold from the chapter at Salisbury to Rome for the canonisation of St Osmund the following year, and he died in Rome having completed his task. Upton's successor was William Fideon, who, it is said, escaped from Constantinople when the Turks finally overthrew the Byzantine Empire in 1453. Settling as a canon of Salisbury, he eventually rebuilt the great hall chamber.

Hemingsby, or Hemyngsby House. A former canonry.

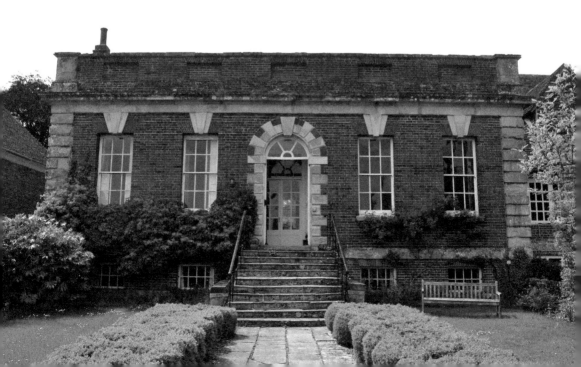

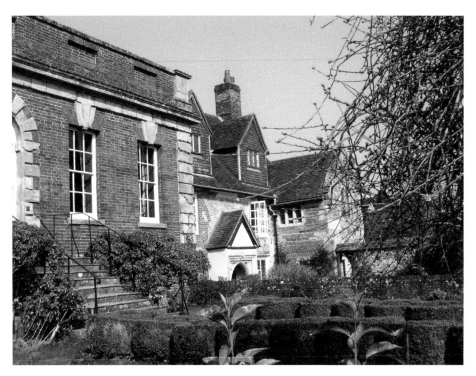

Hemingsby on Cathedral Close.

In 1525, Edward Powell was living at 'Hemyngsby' and acted as counsel to Queen Catherine of Aragon at the hearing of Henry VIII's divorce suit against her. Powell so incurred the king's displeasure that, after Catherine's death, he was tried for treason in London and hanged, drawn and quartered at Smithfield. In the turbulent years of the Reformation that followed, Simon Symonds, the vicar of Bray, in the well-known ballad of that name, lived in the house for three years from 1547.

Although much of the medieval house survives, particularly at the northern end, a major repair had to be carried out to the south end in 1727, which today gives it the appearance of being two houses. Hemingsby ceased to be a canonry in 1846 after the Church Act of 1840 had reduced the number of residentiary canons at Salisbury Cathedral from six to four.

14. Parish of St Lawrence Church

The date of the foundation of this church is uncertain and it is first mentioned as a chapel annexed to St Martin's in Salisbury. The church was said to have been consecrated in 1326, but this may well have been a rebuilt church replacing an earlier one on the site. There is a twelfth-century font, but it is more than possible that this could have originated elsewhere. It is most likely that much of the stone came from the abandoned buildings at Old Sarum. Some features of the chancel are of the thirteenth century and there were alterations and repairs in the fifteenth century. From this period comes the waggon roof, with its interesting carved bosses, probably dating from 1461.

The nave was probably largely rebuilt in the sixteenth century and, in 1711, the tower was rebuilt. In 1553, there were three bells, but one was sold in 1584. In 1998, another of the original bells was sold and five new bells hung, retaining the last original bell (dated 1594) as the treble, making a ring of six.

A survey of St Lawrence by the Royal Commission on Historical Monuments (RCHM), published in 1980, commented on how well the church was maintained and that it was particularly interesting for the many periods represented in its structure, especially for the continued use of a 'medieval' style in the enhancements and improvements in the early 1700s.

Now Grade I listed, such status is only given to buildings of exceptional national interest and historical importance, as they are the cornerstones of our heritage. What makes St Lawrence so special is that its origins go back to the time when it was part of the thriving 'old' Salisbury. Now it is the sole surviving church of that early medieval city. Architecturally and historically, St Lawrence is undoubtedly an important structure that has been looked after continuously, and lovingly, for over 800 years.

St Lawrence Church.

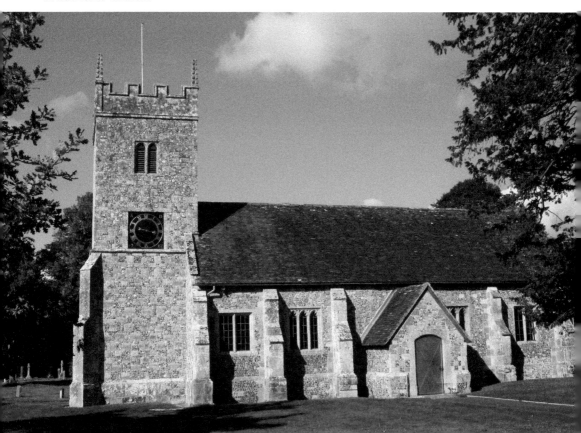

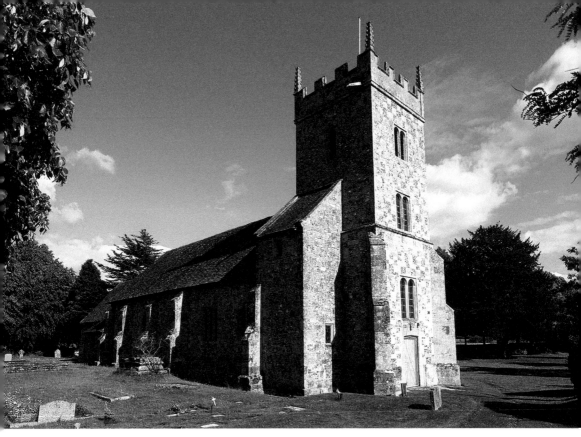

St Lawrence Church. (© Ashley Pomeroy)

15. Haunch of Venison Pub, Minster Street

The Haunch of Venison is one of the oldest hostelries of the region and the first record is *c.* 1320 when the building was used to house craftsmen working on the cathedral spire. Under the fireplace there is a former bread oven with a secure iron gate across it, beyond which is a smoke-preserved, mummified hand. It is believed to be from an eighteenth-century demented whist player who lost it in a card game due to cheating. The hand has been stolen a few times, but now it is securely locked away. When the heating system was changed in the choristers' part of the cathedral, the marble tiles from it were used in the bar to create the unique floor. The 'Horsebox' bar on the ground floor at the front on the right-hand side is referred to as a 'Ladies Snug', dating back to the times where public houses were for men only. The panelled bar counter has a pewter top, which is one of six in the entire country, and there is a rare, wooden, carved, elevated arch with seven original gravity-fed spirit taps fitted in 1909. According to CAMRA there are only five of them left in the United Kingdom. There are no dispensers on the counter and handpumps are affixed to the bar back-fitting, which also has drawers – very rare as well. The 'Horsebox' was reputedly used by Winston Churchill and Dwight Eisenhower during the planning of D-Day landings back in 1944.

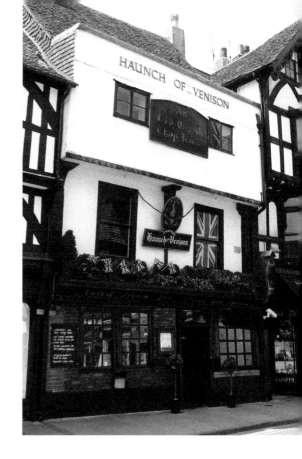

The Haunch of Venison public house.

16. The Old George Inn

The Old George Inn was one of the most important medieval inns in Salisbury. Through a door on the High Street, and the through a maze of offices, fire doors and breeze-block corridors, before you know it you are back in the fifteenth century. The Old George Inn, now perched above the main entrance of the Old George Mall, has been providing bed and board since 1364. But it has been closed to the public since the mid-1990s when its last incarnation, The Bay Tree Restaurant, closed down. Since then, the inn, with its entrance blocked off from the street below, has languished disused, empty and closed to the public. Today you can visit the old inn as part of the annual Heritage Open Days programme. When it opened, it was owned by the Teynturer family. William Teynturer was a member of the Guild of St George, which probably accounts for the inn's name. In 1623, the council decreed that the George was the only place in Salisbury where plays could be staged, 'the size and form of the inner courtyard being well adapted for that purpose'.

As you push open the last fire door, leaving the mall behind you, you enter a remarkable wood-panelled banqueting hall. Trussed together by a forest of pillars and oak beams, the great hall not only boasts a minstrels' gallery but an intricately carved Jacobean mantelpiece.

Above you, on two beam ends, hang two crudely carved figure heads of Edward II and his Queen, Isabella. Queen Isabella, nicknamed 'the she-wolf of France', was fiery to say the least and had her husband done to death, which might explain why they appear to be glaring at each other. The bay window overlooking the high street was built in 1453 at a cost of just £1 by some Italians doing a spot of moonlighting from their work on the cathedral.

But the most impressive part of the Old George Inn has to be its heavyweight celebrity guest list.

In June 1668, diarist Samuel Pepys 'lay in a silke bed' there and had a 'very good diet'. When he 'paid the reckoning', however, he found it 'so exorbitant, and particular in rate of my horses, and 7s. 6d. for bread and beer', he 'was mad, and [resolved] to trouble the mistress about it'. He moved to a cheaper inn the next morning. In 1645, Oliver Cromwell stopped off at the Old George for bed and breakfast on his way to joining the army, and it also crops up in Charles Dickens's novel *Martin Chuzzlewit*. Even William Shakespeare and his strolling players are said to have performed a 'one night stand' in the inn's courtyard, which once stabled up to fifty horses.

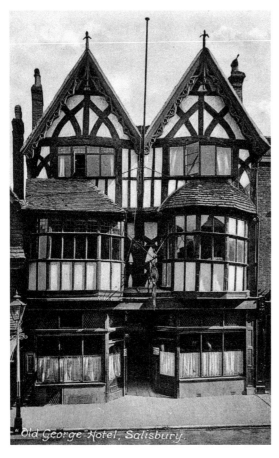

The Old George Hotel.

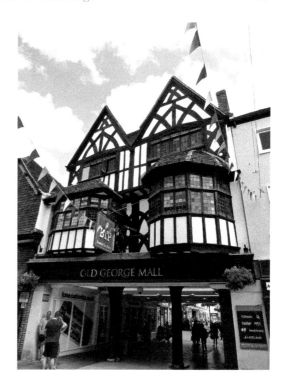

Now the entrance to a shopping mall. (© Glass Angel)

The George also features in H. G. Wells' *Secret Places of the Heart*, in which he alludes to 'the medieval modernity of the Old George smoking-room'. His reverie is interrupted, however, by an American visitor who instructs him to 'just look at that old beam! ... To think it was exactly where it is before there was a Cabot in America!'

It was to this ancient hostelry that Buddy Holly came with the Crickets on 22 March 1958. At the Gaumont that night he was backed by the Tanner Sisters, Gary Miller, Ronnie Keene and his Orchestra, and Des O'Connor. In a letter written from the George to his parents back in Texas, he confided that 'everyone comments on how my jokes get bigger laughs than the comedian on the show, Des O'Connor,' before telling them what a 'real old, quaint place' the George was. Less than twelve months later, he died in a plane crash at the age of twenty-two.

Less than ten years later, in 1967, the ground floor of the George was removed and a steel frame inserted to support the upper floors, creating an arcade into the Old George Mall Shopping Centre.

17. Trinity Hospital Almshouses

The exact date of the foundation of Trinity Hospital is unknown. There is even some conflicting evidence regarding the name of the founder. There seems little doubt, however, that the hospital, built on the site of a former brothel in

New Street, near 'Blackbridge', and dedicated to the Holy Trinity and St Thomas of Canterbury, owes its origin to the munificence of Agnes Bottenham. It is true that a letters patent was issued in 1394 granting John Chandler permission to found the institution, but there is evidence for its existence some years before this. As early as 1379, an indulgence was promised by the Archbishop of Canterbury, together with the bishops of Winchester, Durham, Ely, Lincoln, Salisbury, Exeter, Bath and Wells, Rochester, Hereford and St Asaph, to all those in their dioceses giving assistance to the poor inmates of the hospital of the Holy Trinity and St Thomas Martyr. In 1390, Boniface IX granted the hospital permission to consecrate its chapel and to celebrate Mass and other divine offices therein. Moreover, several of the early records of the hospital specifically refer to Agnes Bottenham as the founder. John Chandler, on the other hand, is mentioned as its master in 1383. He was undoubtedly closely concerned with the well-being of the foundation, both in this capacity and as one of its earliest benefactors. He was, in addition, one of Agnes Bottenham's executors. But there is no evidence that the hospital was rebuilt either on its existing site or on a new one by him.

Provision was made in the hospital for twelve permanently, and eighteen temporarily, resident poor. The latter were allowed to remain a maximum of three

Trinity Hospital Almshouses. (© Graham Tiller)

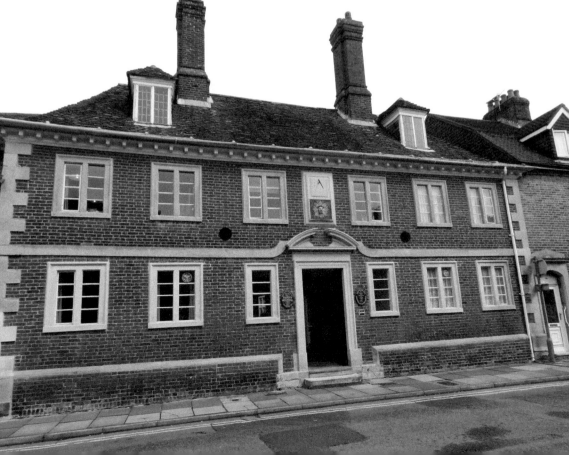

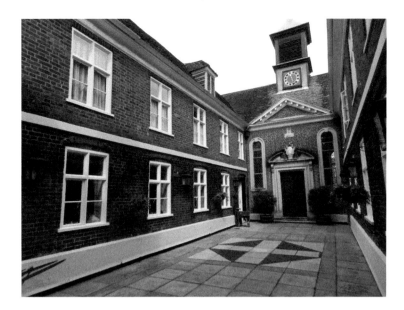

Trinity
Hospital
Almshouses
courtyard.
(© Graham
Tiller)

days and nights except in case of sickness, when they might stay until they recovered. All the needs of the poor were supplied by the subwarden, who was the working head of the institution. He had to be resident and take an oath to carry out his duties faithfully. It was the responsibility of the master to see that he did so, and to remove him, if necessary, after his third offence. In this event the choice of a suitable successor lay with the master. After the death of John Chandler, who kept the office in his own hands during his lifetime, the mastership remained in the hands of the mayor of Salisbury. A resident chaplain celebrated the usual Masses and canonical hours within the hospital, and attendance was compulsory for every inmate.

The history of the hospital witnesses a sincere attempt to carry out the wishes both of its founder and of its earliest benefactor. Indeed, there appears to have been no break in its charitable work. The ordinances have been modified and supplemented, but the foundation has always provided, and is still continuing today, to provide food and shelter for the aged. The wealth and excellent condition of existing records testify to a tradition of sound administration that has resulted in the effective execution of the hospital's work.

18. Braybrooke House

Braybrooke House was once the master's house of the former chorister's school and the residence of Canon Alexander de Hemingsby. Originally Nos 56c and 57 were one building.

It was named after William de Braybrook (1298–1319), executor and beneficiary under the will of Bishop Nicholas Longspee. Some of the rooms in the house during the Middle Ages, such as a hay barn, wine cellar, kitchen and ovens, have been identified from records but nothing about the occupants is known. Dora Robertson, in her history of the cathedral choir school entitled *Sarum Close*, records William Osgodby as having occupied the house in the late fifteenth century. He is said to have entertained, too frequently, Mistress Alicia Hoskyns, an immodest lady of the city, to the misgivings of the Close constable of the time. Dr Thomas Harding, canon treasurer of Salisbury, lived at Braybrooke from 1554 until he was deprived of his office in 1559, for his support of the Roman Catholic Church, and for opposition to Bishop Jewel. In the same year, the dean and chapter granted the house to Christopher Bennet, who became the first in the recorded line of headmasters of the cathedral school. In 1564, schoolmaster John Bold received the house, which was thereafter tied to the office of headmaster.

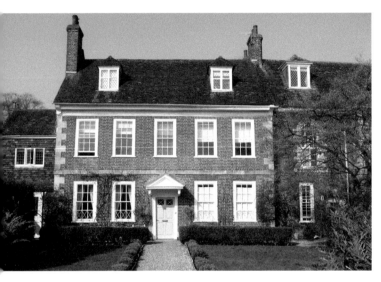

Left: Braybrooke House.

Below: Braybrooke House and the adjacent Wren Hall. (© Tony Hisgett)

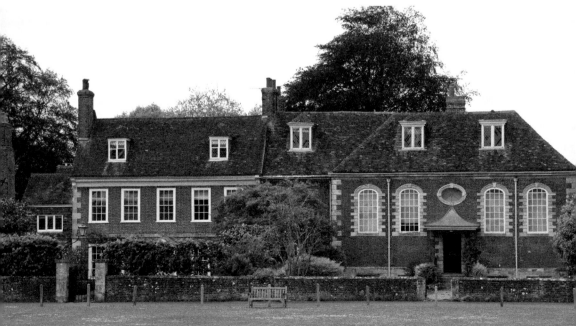

19. Malmesbury House

One of the finest houses in Salisbury is Malmesbury House, which came on the market in 2014, arousing a great deal of interest in this magnificent Grade I listed building. The house is described by *Country Life* as 'one of the finest, oldest and historically most important of the many Grade I listed houses that head up a uniquely picturesque architectural grouping within this green, 80-acre walled enclave at the heart of the city in Wiltshire'. It was placed on the market in excess of £5 million 'for the freehold of the beautifully restored, mainly 18th-century house, which sits tucked away in two thirds of an acre of secure, private gardens adjoining the fourteenth-century St Ann's Gate at the eastern end of the Close'.

Originally known as Copt Hall, a thirteenth-century canonry demolished in 1399 and rebuilt in 1416, Malmesbury House was remodelled by successive generations of the influential Harris family, who leased the house from 1660. It was later renamed in honour of the peripatetic eighteenth-century diplomat James Harris IV, created 1st Earl of Malmesbury in 1800.

The building's elegant Queen Anne front was commissioned by the earl's grandfather, James Harris II, and has been attributed to Sir Christopher Wren, but was most likely the work of local architect John Fort, Wren's master builder. The 1st Earl's father, James Harris III, who inherited a substantial fortune and the house in Cathedral Close on his father's death in 1733, was responsible for the splendid interiors at Malmesbury House. A distinguished politician and classical scholar (although dubbed 'a prig' and a 'coxcomb' by Samuel Johnson), he was also a great lover of music and a close friend of Handel, a regular visitor who is said to have given his first concert in England in the music room above St Ann's Gate, then part of Malmesbury House.

Throughout its history, the house has been a favourite refuge of the great and the good. At the start of the Civil War, Sir George Vaughan, High Sheriff of Wiltshire, was living in the house and it was here that he raised forces in the county to support Charles I. Also in existence is a secret upper room in the orangery, built in 1629, in which Royalists and other dissidents could escape the attention of government forces.

Charles II also stayed at the house, in 1665, when he fled London to avoid the plague. He is said to have addressed the people of Salisbury from the projecting oriel window that overlooks St John Street and bears his coat of arms. Malmesbury House remained a leasehold property owned by the cathedral, before being bought privately by the evangelising Conservative MP John Cordle, who died there in 2004, aged ninety-two.

Bought in 2006, the building was in a fairly poor state of repair and it took a further two years of intensive restoration before they eventually moved in. Few historic buildings can claim to be perfect, but the glorious interiors of Malmesbury House are as close as it gets.

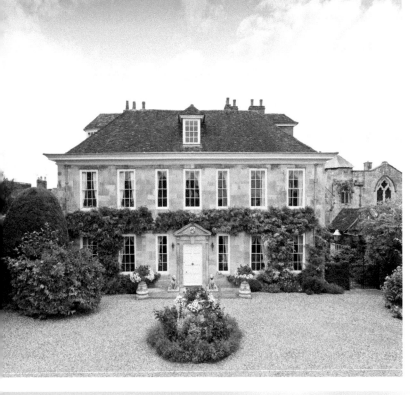

Left: Malmesbury House, named after eighteenth-century diplomat James Harris IV, created 1st Earl of Malmesbury in 1800.

Below: Malmesbury House, restored between 2006 and 2008 after years of neglect.

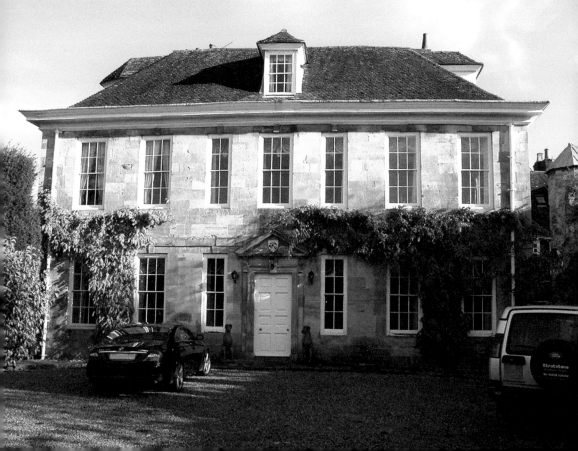

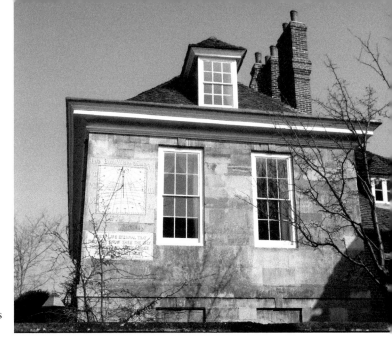

Malmesbury House – 'life's but a walking shadow'.

The classic Queen Anne house is one of Salisbury's gems. Highlights include the grand reception hall and the impressive cantilevered staircase; the well-proportioned drawing room with its painted panelled walls and high ceilings; the dining room with its beautiful fireplace and stuccoed ceiling plasterwork; and the library, one of the most spectacular rooms and a splendid example of Gothic Revival design.

20. The Poultry Cross

Standing proudly at the junction of Silver Street and Minster Street is the Grade I listed Poultry Cross, dating back to the fourteenth century when Salisbury was a thriving market town bringing in lots of business from the surrounding areas. Even now, it plays an integral part of the very popular twice-weekly market in the city.

Erected in around 1450, it was modified in the eighteenth century. The site had previously housed a high cross that had been in place since 1307. The structure is a hexagonal, open, arched shelter with buttressed piers enriched with carved and panelled pinnacles. A central stone shaft with a stone seat round at the base, it was originally finished with a sundial block. The flying buttresses were added in 1850 by a local stonemason who was jealous of a similar cross in Chichester, and the cross was originally surrounded by a square of stone seats that have since been removed. Drawings of the original cross are displayed in Salisbury Museum.

The tradition of market crosses being used to designate the site of a market or fair dates back to the seventh century. The right to hold a market was granted by the monarch, a bishop or a baron, and most market towns in Britain have such a cross. There were originally four market crosses in Salisbury, including the Poultry Cross, which is the only one that remains: the Cheese Cross in the Cheesemarket

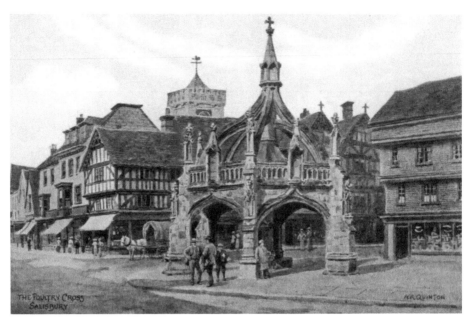

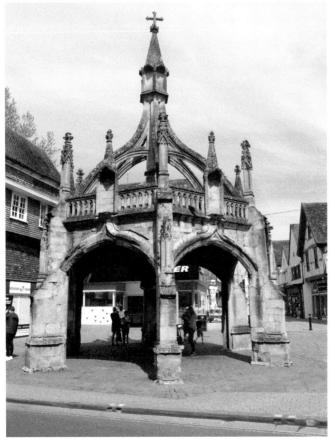

Above: The Poultry Cross.

Left: The Grade I listed Poultry Cross, a major landmark in Salisbury.

area of the town; Barnard's Cross, which indicated the livestock market at the junction of Barnard Street and Culver Street; and one in Market Place, near the war memorial, which designated the wool and yarn market.

21. Odeon Cinema, New Canal, The Hall of John Halle

The striking medieval building that now houses the Odeon Cinema was once the home of a well-known local wool merchant, the wealthy John Halle. It was built in 1470s but Halle died in 1479 and the building was finished by his son William years later.

The foyer boasts impressive dark oak beams, beautiful stained-glass windows, wrought-iron chandeliers and a very large stone fireplace. The building also houses a Grade I listed banqueting hall.

Halle was a colourful character and very involved in local politics. He served as local councillor in 1446, became an alderman in 1448 and, in 1449, he was constable of New Street Ward before being finally elected mayor in 1451. To crown his achievements, he was Salisbury's first elected Member of Parliament in 1453, which was repeated three times. Despite his commitment to serving the town, he was sent to the Tower of London by Edward IV because of his aggressive behaviour over a land dispute with the bishop of Salisbury and other local landowners. Curiously, Halle was elected mayor for a fourth time while he was still in the Tower, mainly because the residents disliked the bishop!

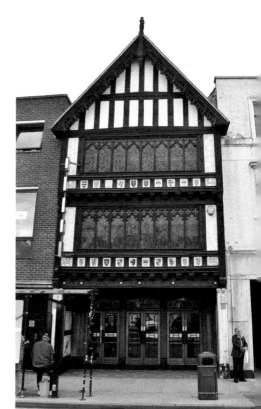

The wonderfully preserved Hall of John Halle, now a cinema. (© Ben Abel)

In 1931, the building was converted into a theatre called the Gaumont Palace before being renamed 'The Gaumont' in 1936. In 1964, it became the Odeon and stars of the time such as the Rolling Stones, the Beatles, the Bee Gees and Buddy Holly played there. The cinema was so popular with locals that when it was threatened with closure in 1986, there was a campaign to save it. It was duly refurbished, using original paints and plasterwork, with the addition of extra screens and a restaurant.

22. Aula le Stage, No. 21 The Close

An unusually named house, Aula le Stage, is built of knapped flint and is one of the most complex buildings in the city. From the early beginnings of the city some of the canons dwelt along the North Walk and Bishop's Walk. In the former, one of the earliest houses is that known as 'Aula le Stage' in documents dating from the early fifteenth century – now No. 21. The name derives from the house having an upper storey and a tower. It was one of the four houses in the Close to possess its own chapel, to which probably belonged the thirteenth-century single-light lancets still to be seen. The chief internal alterations took place in the sixteenth century and the front was rebuilt in the eighteenth century. Between 1531 and 1581, the occupiers of Aula le Stage leased the grounds of a house called Loders at

Aula le Stage, on the Close.

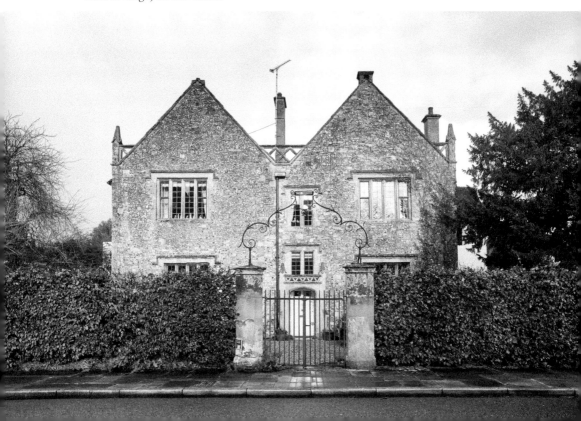

its rear, which was the prebendal mansion of the abbey of St Mary, Montebourg, Normandy, the parent house of the priory of Loders and chapel of Bradpole, both in Dorset. Aula le Stage was large enough to provide an occasional meeting place for the cathedral chapter. The list of its canonical residents is known from 1316 to 1850, after which date it has been in lay occupation. Three of the early canons had houses along Bishop's Walk, one being on the site of the present deanery and diocesan registry.

23. The Rifles Berkshire and Wiltshire Museum – The Wardrobe

The original building on this site was constructed in 1254. It was rebuilt in the fifteenth century and was used to store the robes of the bishop of Salisbury, hence it was known as the 'Bishop's Wardrobe' or 'The Wardrobe'. It has been radically altered over the years, but retains much of its thirteenth-century masonry carcass of a classic H-shaped hall house. The central open hall was flanked by two-storey cross wings at either end. Built of flint brick and stone rubble, with stone quoins, it is now a military museum.

The Wardrobe, now a local museum.

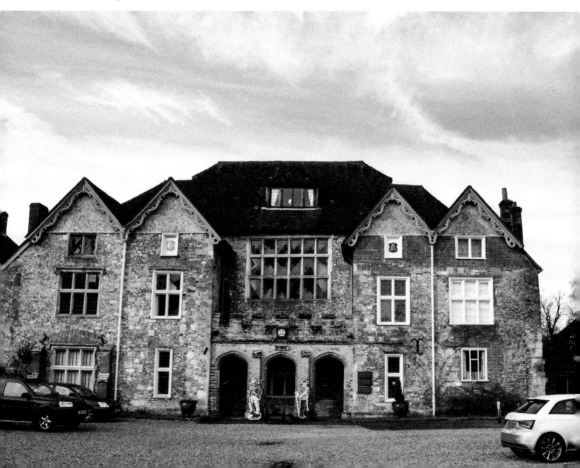

24. Mill House and the Old Mill

The Old Mill is a late fifteenth- or early sixteenth-century building with features dating back to 1250. It has been a mill for many centuries but never ground corn, and was almost certainly used for fulling – a process in woolen clothmaking that involves the cleansing of cloth (particularly wool) to eliminate oils, dirt and other impurities, and to make it thicker.

The current building was converted in the sixteenth century from ecclesiastical use into Wiltshire's first paper mill, when the River Nadder was diverted to flow under it, and in later years it was used as a yarn factory and as a bone mill. The southern end of the building, which houses the public bar, did not exist in 1808

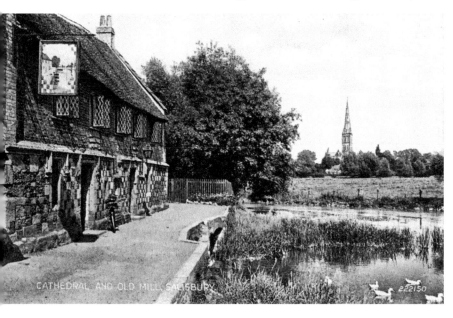

The Mill House and Old Mill with cathedral in the distance.

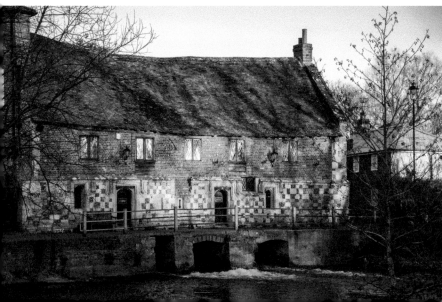

One of the most picturesque scenes locally.

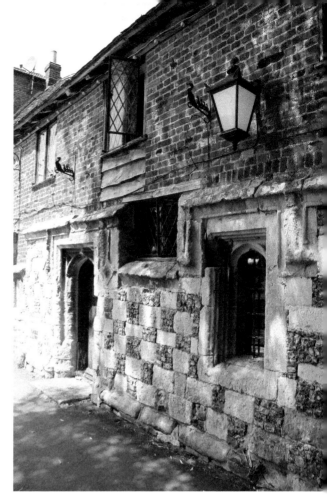

Right: The Old Mill. (© Steve Everett)

Below: The Old Mill, Harpham.
(© Gordon Oliver)

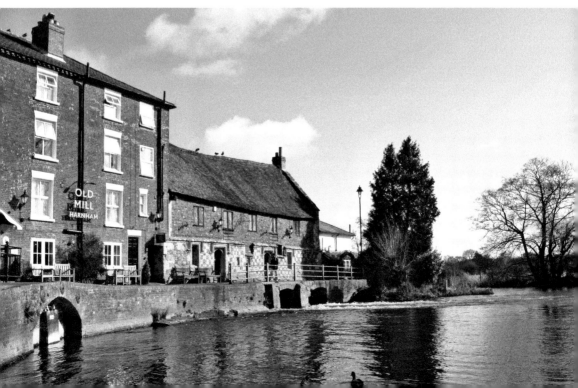

but is present by 1834. In the early twentieth century the property was converted into a country club by Mary Fox-Pitt, daughter-in-law of Augustus Pitt Rivers. The atmosphere was praised by the food writer Florence White, author of *Good Things in England* (1932). She quotes the artist Augustus John, saying, 'It is the best cookery in England.' The mill has a very picturesque setting, looking over a large pool down the river.

25. Church House and Former Workhouse, Crane Street

This former workhouse was built on Crane Street in the fifteenth century for William Lightfoot, a wealthy clothier. In 1630, the house was sold to Sir Mervyn Touchet, Lord Audley and Earl of Castlehaven, who named it Audley House, a name perpetuated in the next-door property. Following his execution on Tower Hill for high crimes in 1634, the house was sold and eventually became a workhouse in 1638. In 1770, the Salisbury parishes of St Edmund, St Martin and St Thomas were incorporated under a local Act of Parliament. The Incorporation had powers to set up a Board of Guardians for the administration of poor relief and other matters, and to operate a workhouse, which it continued to do at Crane Street.

Because of its local Act status, Salisbury was exempt from most of the provisions of the 1834 Poor Law Amendment Act. The Incorporation continued in operation until 1869 when it was dissolved along with a number of similar bodies. The city's parishes then joined the surrounding Alderbury Poor Law Union. By the early 1880s the building was under threat of demolition. A report of 1881 describes the house at that time:

> About a year ago the antiquarian world was shocked at an advertisement issued by the Town Council of Salisbury offering the ancient building, which had for some time served as the city workhouse, for sale, with the condition appended that the purchaser should pull the building down and erect something new on its site … Audley House, or the Old Workhouse at Salisbury was erected during the fifteenth century … that which faces the street is the most ancient … the buildings facing the river are of later date and were probably erected at various times between the reigns of James I and Charles II. They are remarkably picturesque and the grouping of gables, chimneys, and roofs, all crowned by the distant spire of the cathedral, makes up a very pretty picture.

Thankfully, Thomas Sanctuary, the Archdeacon of Dorset, purchased the house in 1881 and renovated it for use as a diocesan church house. Today it is called Church House.

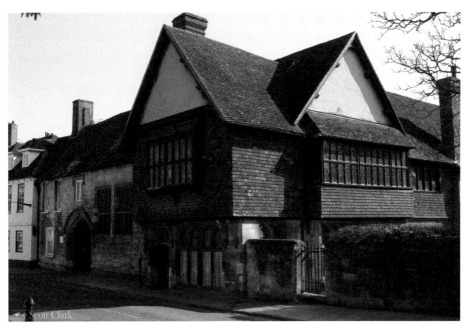

Church House, once a workhouse and dates from the fifteenth century.

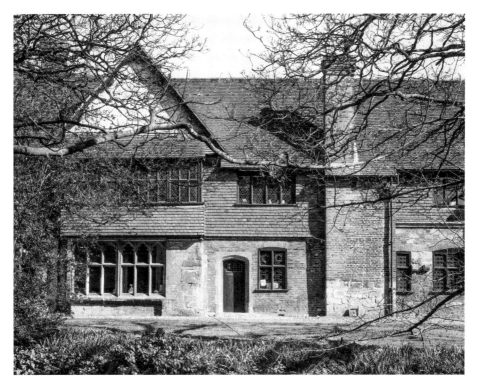

Once threatened with demolition, now restored and is the Diocesan Church House.

26. The Joiners' Hall

The Joiners' Hall was built as a meeting house for the Joiners' Guild around 1612 and is one of three major examples of timber framework on a large scale from the early seventeenth century in Salisbury. It is an impressive building with the façade decorated with elaborately carved timberwork. The main survivals from the seventeenth century are the four remarkable external walls, in particular the façade with its two exceptional, double-transomed first-floor windows on grotesque brackets and its carved fascia.

The building's former glory has been described in further detail in historical records: 'The Joiners' Hall was on the first floor … and entrance was by the left-hand door on the street. The other door led to a tenement at street level, presumably occupied by a caretaker. The walls of the hall originally presented "one uniform surface of the most minute and exquisite carving on panel with corinthian pilasters".' The carvings and corbels of the exterior are thought to have been done by the Salisbury joiner and carver Humphrey Beckham. Beckham's craftsmanship had made him rich, but he appears to have lived frugally to the ripe old age of eighty-three. Look closely at the six humanoid figures that grace the front of the building. Instead of the more usual gargoyles or animals, they consist of five unmistakably male heads, but surmounting five unmistakably female bodies. The heads are realistic in style and differ from each other sufficiently to suggest that they are carvings of actual characters. The female bodies, on the other hand, are grotesque to the point of near obscenity.

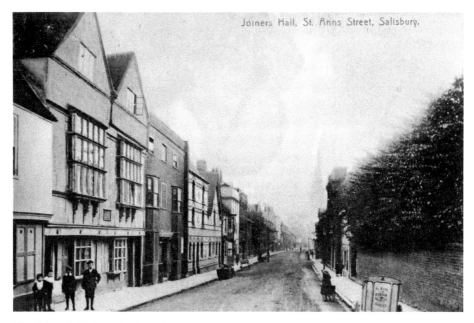

The Joiners' Hall on St Anns Street.

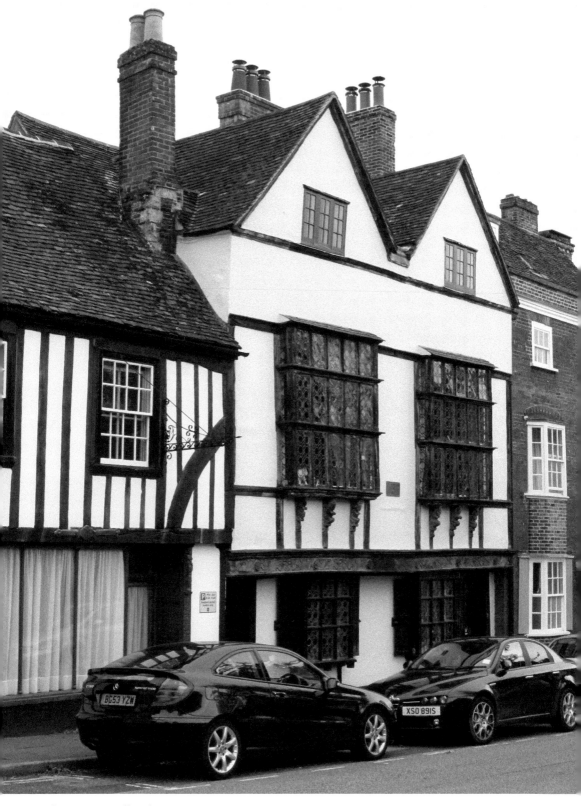

The Joiners' Hall today.

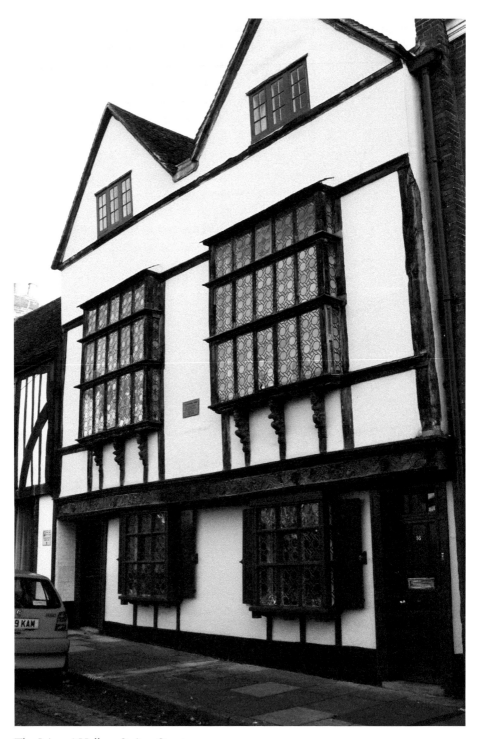

The Joiners' Hall on St Ann Street.

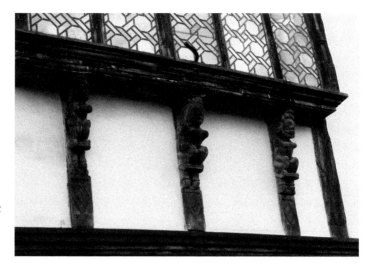

Grotesque
carvings of
bewhiskered
figures with
enormous breasts,
found on the front
of the Joiners'
Hall on St Ann
Street.

Why did Humphrey do this? A traditional belief is that he fell out with six of
the city aldermen, or with leading members of the guild. Did he then insultingly
caricature them as women for posterity? An acceptable insult, of course, in
the 1600s.

In the nineteenth century the lower storey of the north front was remodelled
and the interior of the building was extensively altered when a partition
and fireplaces were inserted, making two houses. The Joiner's decided to sell
their hall in 1842 and, in 1850, it was sold to Messrs Griffin and Wolferstan
and then sold by them to Charles Trim and A. C. Rhoades. In 1893, the hall
was bought by Mr Arthur Whitehead and was placed under the care of the
National Trust. The Trust acquired the property in 1898 and had it repaired
and restored.

27. The White Hart Hotel

The White Hart is a Grade II* listed building and has recognised historical and
architectural interest at a national level. The present building is largely late
eighteenth or early nineteenth century in date, replacing a former inn of the
same name. The plan form of the older parts of the building reflects the original
accommodation for guests and their transport, with the older parts of the hotel
building having significant levels of design value. The scale, style and ambition of
the building were clearly intended to distinguish it from surrounding structures,
and although this has been compromised by some more recent building within its
immediate setting, it is still clearly identifiable as a purpose-built historic hotel.
The hotel remains in its original use. There has been an inn of this name on the site
since at least 1635.

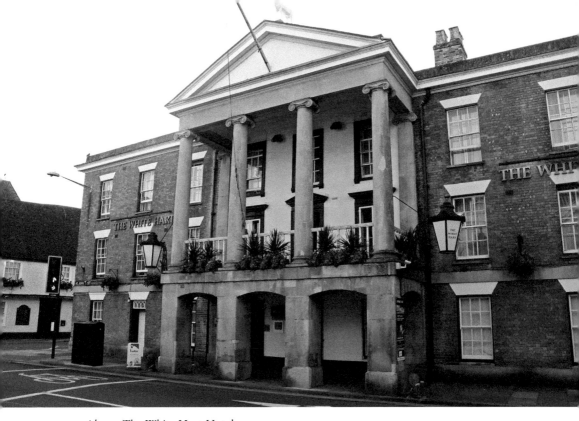

Above: The White Hart Hotel.

Below: The White Hart Hotel, somewhat out of keeping in Salisbury but architecturally important.

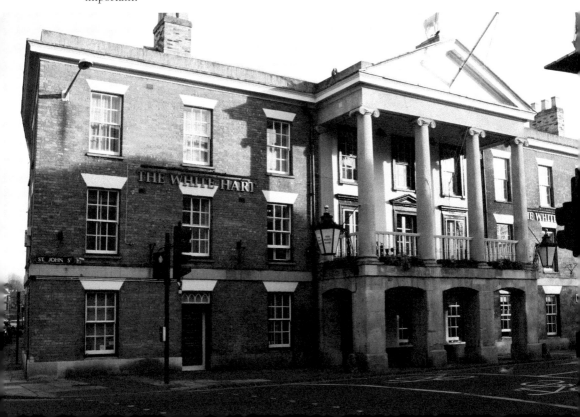

28. The College of Matrons

Almshouses are charitable housing provided to enable people to live in a particular community. They are often targeted at the poor of a locality, at those from certain forms of previous employment or their widows, and are generally maintained by a charity or the trustees of a bequest. They tend to be characterised by the aim of supporting the continued independence of their residents.

Many almshouses are Christian institutions, though some are secular. They trace their history back to monastic times where the terms bedehouse, hospital, maison dieu, almshouse and others described the provision of accommodation for those in need. The first recorded almshouse was founded by King Athelstan in York in the tenth century, and the oldest still in existence is thought to be the Hospital of St Oswald in Worcester, which dates from *c.* 990. By the middle of 1500s there were around 800 medieval hospitals spread across the country, but following the dissolution of the monasteries only a handful remained, and these were refounded on secular lines and rebuilt in the new domestic collegiate style. Thus, many almshouses are typified by the traditional three-sided square that provide a sense of safety and security without isolating residents from the outside world.

Of the 1,700 groups of almshouse charities today, over 30 per cent occupy listed buildings and many have celebrated anniversaries of over 400 years. Another feature of this rich heritage is that many almshouses lie in the heart of towns and villages, ensuring that they remain closely integrated in the local community, with the added benefit of ensuring residents are close to shops and services.

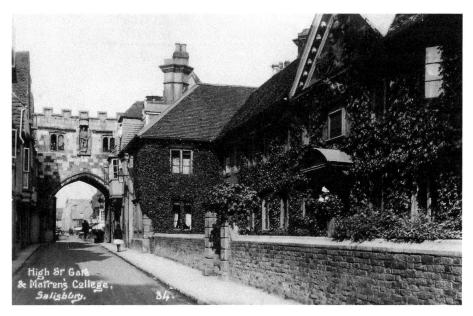

High Street gates and Matron's College.

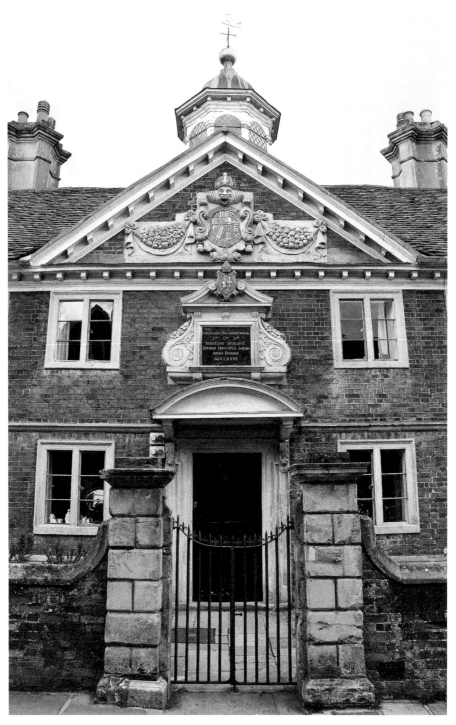

The Grade I listed Matron's College, constructed in 1685 by Seth Ward as an almshouse for ten widows of clergy ordained within the diocese of Salisbury. (© Ben Abel)

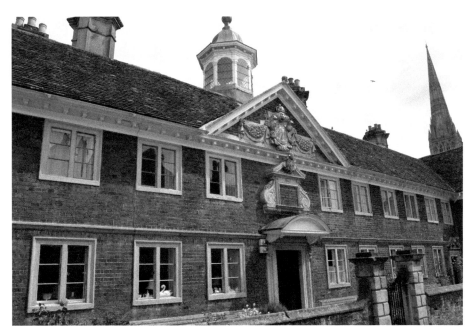

The Matron's College.

There is an important delineation between almshouses and other forms of sheltered housing in that almshouse residents are beneficiaries, rather than tenants, of the charity. As such, they reside in the accommodation under a licence to occupy.

The College of Matrons almshouses were founded here in 1683 by Seth Ward, the bishop of Salisbury. At the time applicants to the College of Matrons had to fulfil certain conditions. 'Matrons shall be needy and deserving single women … preference being given to widows and daughters of Ministers of the Church of England.' The college remains an almshouse, and still with the same criteria for eligibility.

There is some uncertainty about whether Sir Christopher Wren designed the building. The wall and gates are Grade I listed separately from the house. The building was extended and renovated in 1870.

29. Sarum College (Theological College)

From the early Middle Ages, Salisbury was an important centre for theological training, its great cathedral and Cathedral Close attracting students and scholars from across Europe.

The history of theological study begins with St Osmund and the completion of the first cathedral at Old Sarum in 1092. After Old Sarum was abandoned in favour of New Sarum and the new cathedral was built in the 1220s, several colleges were established as well as a medieval school of theology here on the site of No. 19 The Close.

The oldest part of Sarum College is the main building at the front of the site, which was built in 1677. Attributed to Sir Christopher Wren, it was built for Francis Hill, a distinguished London lawyer and deputy recorder for Salisbury. He chose a particularly striking site at the north end of Bishop's Walk, facing directly down to the Bishop's Palace, now the Cathedral School.

The establishment of the theological college in 1860 began with a gift. Walter Kerr Hamilton, bishop of Salisbury used an anonymous donation to buy the house (then No. 87) from Miss Charlotte Wyndham – and the first students arrived in January 1861.

In the 1870s, William Butterfield, foremost church architect of his day, and best known for Keble College, Oxford, was commissioned to add a residential wing to provide accommodation for students, and then, in 1881, a chapel and library. In 1937, further extensions designed by William Randall Blacking were added, study bedrooms for students and a meeting room that became the new library and which is now the Common Room.

During the Second World War the college was taken over by the women of the Auxiliary Territorial Service, the women's branch of the British Army, and Queen Mary paid them a visit. Apparently, the creepers that covered the front of the building were hastily removed, as the queen did not like them.

In October 1971, the two theological colleges in Salisbury and Wells merged and became Salisbury & Wells Theological College. The additional students

Sarum College and former Theological College.

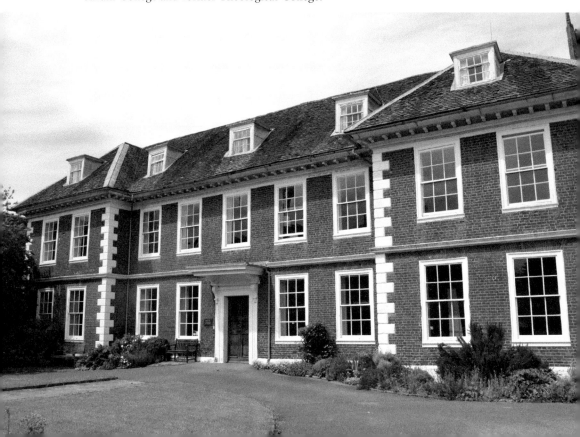

required more space, and two further extensions were built: a three-storey block of flats and study bedrooms at the eastern end of the Butterfield building (the East Wing), and a new chapel (now the Royal School of Church Music's administrative centre), refectory and library were added.

By 1994, the Salisbury & Wells College had closed, and the following year Sarum College was established to provide ecumenical theological education, including courses, conferences, events and hospitality, as well as a home for ministerial training.

Work to restore and improve the buildings continued and in 2006 the new link building, joining the 1677 and 1877 buildings and incorporating lift access, won the 2006 Salisbury Civic Society's Conservation award.

30. Mompesson House

There has long been a house on the site here on Cathedral Close; however, the current Mompesson House is around 300 years old and was named after Charles Mompesson, for whom it was built in 1701. The hopper heads at the top of the downpipes bear the initials 'CM' and the date of construction.

The Mompessons were an old Wiltshire family, recorded from the early fifteenth century. Several of them had been sheriffs. Charles's father, Sir Thomas, an ardent royalist, was an MP and Charles was himself an MP for some years – one of two for the rotten borough of Old Sarum, which had an electorate of only ten.

The situation of Mompesson on the north side of Chorister's Green in Cathedral Close made it a very desirable place for the Mompessons to live. Originally, the houses here had been intended for the clergy to live in, but by the mid-seventeenth century it became very fashionable for local gentry and professional classes to live there. In 1703, Charles Mompesson married Elizabeth Longueville and their union was celebrated with the addition of a decorative cartouche above the front door – their new joint coat of arms.

Charles Mompesson died in 1714 and his brother-in-law Charles Longueville took over the lease on the house soon after. It is him we have to thank for the richly decorated interiors; he commissioned the magnificent plasterwork and the oak staircase in the 1740s and raised the height of the ceiling in the large drawing room.

Following in the footsteps of the Mompessons and Charles Longueville, successive families took over the lease on the house: the Hayters to 1800, the Portmans to 1843 and the Townsends to 1939. They each took possession of an empty house, moved in, bringing their furniture and belongings with them, created their home and made modest changes to the interiors (generally just a simple coat of paint in the fashion of the time). When they moved out they took all their personal effects, furniture and belongings with them. As a result, the collection you see when you visit Mompesson today contains very few indigenous items. Those that remain are treasured and many relate to Barbara Townsend, who lived at Mompesson for almost a century. Her family moved into the house in 1843 when she was a young child and she lived there until her death in 1939. She was a self-taught artist and recorded everyday life in Cathedral Close and family excursions further afield. She worked mainly in watercolour and produced a huge number of paintings during her long life. She also decorated cups, plates and tiles. Barbara Townsend was very happy with Mompesson as it was – in all its unmodernised splendor – and so it is largely due to her that it survived into the twentieth century in its unchanged and intact condition.

After Barbara Townsend's death, the dean and chapter of Salisbury Cathedral sold the freehold of the house to the Church Commissioners. The house temporarily acted as the official home for the bishop of Salisbury, but it proved to be unsuitable so the Church Commissioners decided that the house would be sold.

Denis Martineau was a London-based architect who was looking to buy a cottage in Wiltshire to use as a weekend retreat. Mompesson was drawn to his attention when it appeared as an advertisement in *Country Life* magazine in 1952. After considerable negotiation, Martineau arranged to buy the house from the Church Commissioners; a condition of the sale was that he agreed to give the property to the National Trust on his death.

Martineau died in 1975 and, contrary to expectations, he did not leave the contents of the house to the National Trust. Suddenly, the National Trust had

Mompesson House, now owned by the National Trust.

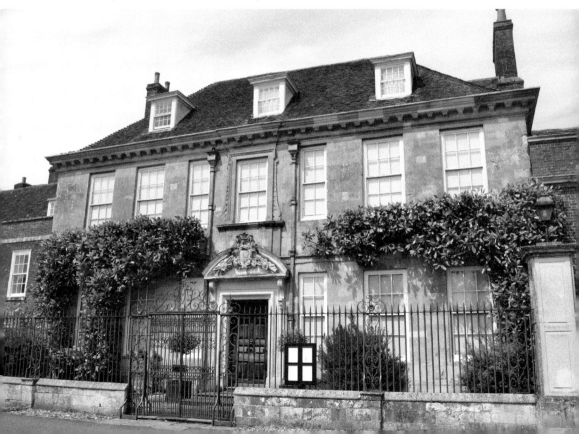

to decide the future of the empty house. In April 1976, it was decided that the principal rooms of the house were to be redecorated, furnished and opened to visitors, and Mompesson officially opened on 1 May 1977.

31. Wren Hall

Wren Hall is a Grade I listed building in Cathedral Close and is situated on the west side of Choristers' Green and was originally part of the attached Braybrook House. A rebuilding was commissioned and funded by Sir Stephen Fox, a former pupil of the Cathedral School and carried out in 1714 by Thomas Naish, who was clerk of works to the cathedral, to provide a classroom and further dormitories for the cathedral choristers. The foundation of the school is thirteenth century. Alexander de Hemmingsby is the first custos of the school on record. He was canon from 1304 to 1334 and lived in the adjoining Braybrooke House. The building here has little, if any, connection with Sir Christopher Wren, except that in its style it provides a suitable memorial to the Wiltshire-born architect.

Wren Hall, with no connection to the great Wiltshire-born architect.

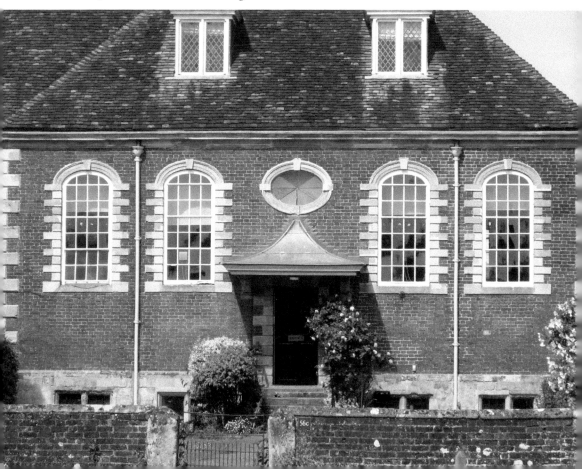

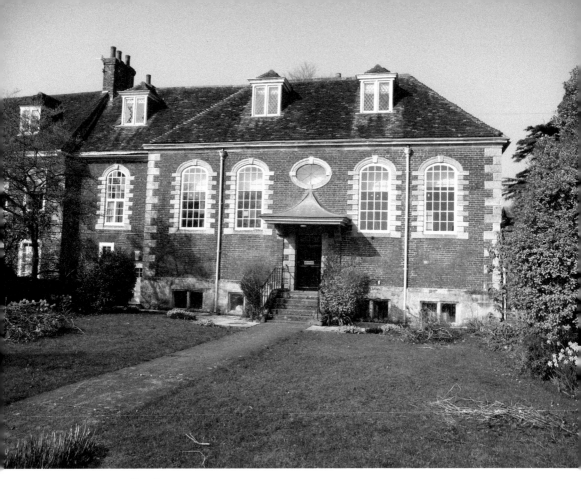

Wren Hall today.

After the removal of the choir school, the College of Sarum St Michael acquired it for a short period until it became the diocesan archive repository. In the 1980s, it was used as the Salisbury Cathedral Spire Appeal office and later became a cathedral educational resource centre for school visits. The desks of the headmaster and assistant master remain at opposite ends of the room as a reminder of the original use as a single large classroom, or 'Big School Room' as it was called, with the two classes sitting back-to-back. The attic contains some dormitories and there are original medieval cellars below the building.

32. The Walton Canonry

The Walton Canonry is an outstanding Grade I listed house, which, in its current guise, is believed to date from around 1720. This replaced an older medieval building that was on the same site, documented as early as 1313. It is an exquisite example of early Georgian architecture with its beautiful symmetry and fine period detail. The house is constructed of deep rose-coloured brick with

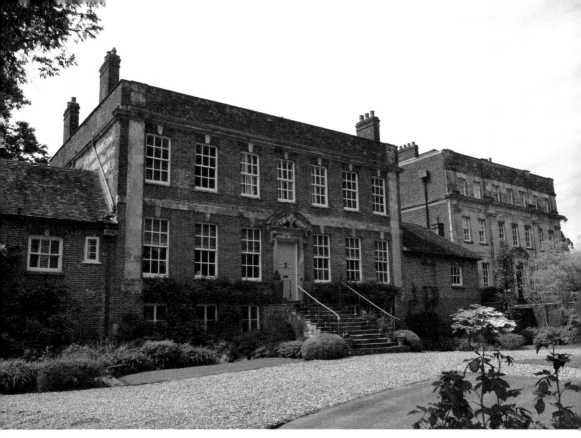

The Walton Canonry and a fine example of early Georgian architecture in Salisbury.

stone bands under a tile roof. The earlier house was occupied by Canon Isaac Walton, who was the son of the renowned fisherman and author Isaak Walton. Isaak Walton was the author of the iconic *The Compleat Angler*, which was first published in 1653. Walton was the last inhabitant of the medieval building and it is after him the building is named. The Walton Canonry has strong artistic connections and one of its occupiers was the artist Rex Whistler, who lived there from 1938 until his untimely death in 1944. The house is still sometimes referred to as 'The Whistler House'. The renowned artist John Constable was a regular visitor here after his close personal friend, the bishop of Salisbury, commissioned him for another painting, *Salisbury Cathedral from The Bishop's Grounds*. He later created the more dramatic painting from the meadow with an ominous sky that many art experts believe reflected the turbulent state of his life at the time.

33. No. 68 Myles Place

No. 68 Myles Place is often described as the stateliest eighteenth-century house in Cathedral Close. The house is said to have been built between 1718 and 1720 on the site of an early canonical house, known in the sixteenth century as Myles

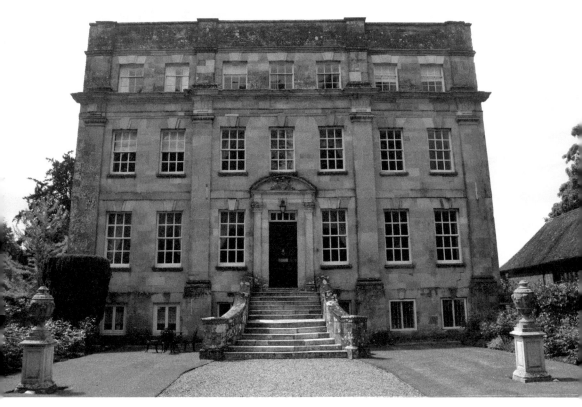

No. 68 Myles Place almost looks out of place on Cathedral Close.

Place. It is now Grade I listed. It is ashlar faced with brick on the sides and at the back, and consists of seven bays with a three-bay centre. The historian Sir Arthur Bryant lived there after the Second World War until his death in 1985.

34. Godolphin School

Godolphin was founded in 1726 from a bequest made by Elizabeth Godolphin (1663–1726) 'for the better education and maintenance of eight young gentlewomen to be brought up at Sarum or some other town in the County of Wilts under the care and direction of some wise and prudent Governess or Schoolmistress'.

The dean and chapter, having refused to act as trustees of this property, invested the money under the authority of the Court of Chancery, but nothing was done to put Elizabeth's scheme into operation until 1784. In that year the Godolphin School was opened in Rosemary Lane in Cathedral Close, but it was not until March 1831 that the full number of eight orphan gentlewomen was entered, in addition to private pupils who could be admitted at the will of the headmistress. The original task of the school was to teach the girls to dance, work, read, write, cast accounts and become proficient in housewifery. The curriculum was enlarged during the nineteenth century to include French, Geography and music.

The school remained in Cathedral Close for fifty-four years, occupying Arundel's House and King's House, but in 1848, owing to an outbreak of cholera in the city, the school moved to Shady Bower, to the house now known as Milford Grove, 'with great benefit to the pupils' health'.

So far the school had been housed in the private residence of the headmistress, but the time had come for the erection of a school building to be the property of the trustees; accordingly, in 1867, 'Fawcett House' was completed and the little school was installed there and given the name of Godolphin School.

Another innovation at the same time was the admission of day girls, though few at first seem to have taken advantage of the permission. By 1876, the numbers outgrew the accommodation and plans were made to purchase a site on Milford Hill and build a new and larger school there.

In January 1890, the school passed into the hands of Mary Alice Douglas, who is considered its second founder. Under her, the present school building was opened in October 1891, consisting of the present hall and two classrooms on either side. During her thirty years as headmistress Miss Douglas saw the numbers increase to 230 and was responsible for many notable additions to the original building.

In 1904, an additional 6 acres were purchased in order to extend the school grounds, which were then landscaped on the Laverstock-facing side; in 1914, the oak panelling, which gives the hall its unique atmosphere, was installed;

Godolphin School.

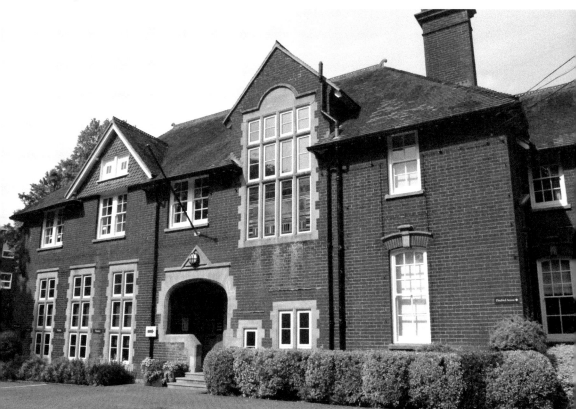

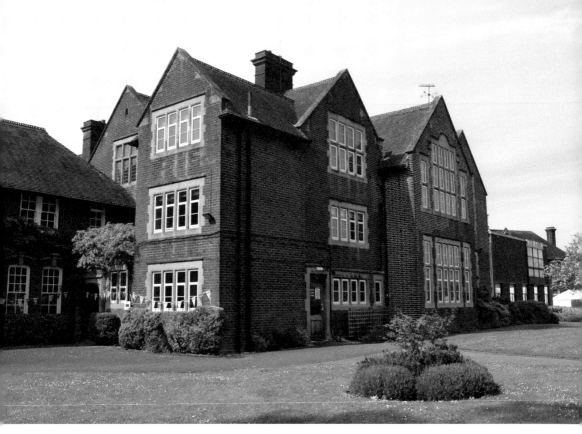

A popular school today.

and in 1925, an open-air swimming pool was opened. Post-war additions to the school have included a library block, several new boarding houses, a science and technology block, a prep school, a performing arts centre, an indoor swimming pool with fitness centre, a new boarding house (Cooper) and a Sixth Form Centre.

Miss Douglas was one of the great pioneers in the education of girls and her belief in the right use of freedom, in the absence of petty rules, and in self-discipline has left its impression on the school for all time.

35. Wesleyan Chapel, Church Street

When John Wesley paid the first of his many visits to Salisbury in 1738, he found a bustling city that provided a natural centre for trade from the surrounding countryside.

In 1736, Westley Hall, John Wesley's brother-in-law, came to the city as a curate at Fisherton Anger. He lived with his wife in Fisherton Street and it was there that John Wesley visited his mother who was staying at the house in February 1738. He came again in June to tell his mother about the momentous religious experience he had undergone on 24 May, and by 1741 the foundations for the new Methodist work were taking shape. There followed a domestic row in 1748 when Westley Hall and John Wesley disagreed. During the next two years a small group of Methodists met above a shop in Greencroft Street. John Wesley preached there in 1750 and the first Methodist society in central southern England was established.

This was obviously not a suitable venue and so a plot of land was purchased in St Edmund's Church Street in 1758. An indenture for the land was assigned to John Wesley and local businessmen. The plot had on it two messuages, or tenements and gardens. This new building was erected in the gardens behind the dwellings. The indenture for the land was signed by seven local men and was leased for 1,000 years at an annual rent of one peppercorn.

St Edmund's Church Street is in Griffin Chequer, which at that time was in the poor end of the city. There was a water ditch down one side of the street, and it was the most easterly chequer to have this. The next chequer further north is Vanners Chequer, which was poorer still.

John Wesley recorded in his journal his pleasure with the new meeting house and described it as 'the most complete in England. It strikes everyone of any taste that sees it, not with any singular part but an inexpressible something in the whole'.

In September 1759, when the chapel was opened, Wesley preached there. The Hampshire Militia were in town and their behaviour was so disruptive that Wesley commented, 'such brutish behaviour have I seldom seen'. Over the next few years, Wesley visited Salisbury almost annually, usually during the first week in October.

Francis Asbury became the superintendent minister on the Salisbury circuit in 1770. The circuit then covered a large area stretching from Chichester to Shaftesbury, including the Isle of Wight. We do not know how often he preached at the chapel in St Edmund's Church Street, but he attended the conference of John Wesley's preachers in Bristol in 1771 and responded to his appeal for missionaries to go to America. He was one of the two ministers chosen and has often been called 'The Father of American Methodism', becoming its first bishop.

In the 1780s, Captain Thomas Webb, one of the most colourful of early Methodists, added impetus to the growth of the congregation. He had been converted in Bristol in 1764 and had been to America, bringing back a picture of the Methodist fire spreading through the New Lands. His preaching was remarked on by Wesley in August 1785: 'On Saturday 13th I went on to Salisbury. As Captain Webb had just been there, I endeavoured to avail myself of the fire which he seldom fails to kindle. The congregation in the evening was very large and seemed to be greatly affected.'

On 27 September 1790, John Wesley preached in Salisbury for the last time. In his journal he says of the occasion: 'I do not know that ever I saw the house so crowded before with high and low, rich and poor.'

There is no record of what the first Methodist chapel looked like in St Edmund's Church Street, but it was demolished in 1810 and a new classical building erected, which still forms the core of the church. It has been enlarged and altered in stages. The new building cost £3,920 and was opened on 26 June 1811. An interesting account of the opening is given in the *Salisbury and Winchester Journal* of 1 July 1811:

> On Wednesday last the newly erected Methodist Chapel in this City was opened for Divine Service. Appropriate and impressive discourses were delivered in the morning and evening by the Rev Joseph Benson, of London; the Rev J Chettle of Southampton preached in the afternoon; and the Rev T Newton of Southampton and Rev H Cheverton of Newbury assisted in the services of the day. The congregations were numerous and respectable, and the collection at the door amounted to £77.

The church in St Edmund's Church Street was altered in 1870, towers were added and a semicircular colonnaded front and the west front was rendered, and a pulpit installed. Further changes were made, especially during financially troubling times and dwindling numbers in the 1950s. However, today, after

Wesleyan Chapel on Church Street.

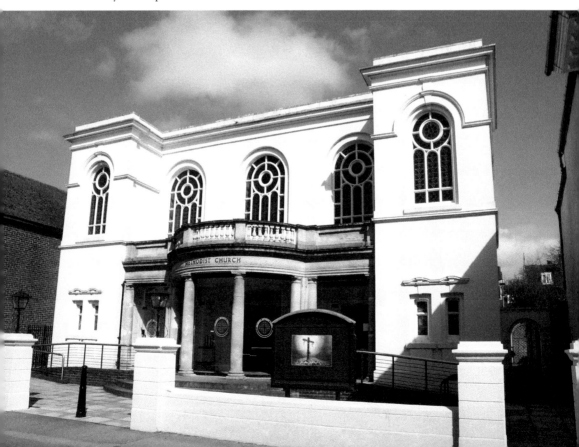

further restoration, the redesigned spaces of the sanctuary, hall and meeting rooms now provide facilities to further the mission of the church and to grow in the community.

36. Former Salisbury Infirmary

The Salisbury Infirmary had a long history as a hospital. The 1st Lord Feversham, who died in 1763, left a sum of £500 towards the establishment of a county hospital, and at a general meeting on 23 September 1766 a committee was established. The Earl of Pembroke was nominated as visitor, the Earl of Radnor as president and Robert Cooper as treasurer, while Dr Henry Hele and Dr Jacob were appointed as physicians.

A site was purchased and the existing houses on it were opened for the reception of patients on 2 May 1767. Meanwhile, plans were drawn up by John Wood the Younger of Bath for a new four-storey building on the site with over 100 beds. When the new red-brick building was completed and opened in 1771 the existing houses were removed. The hospital was later much enlarged, with a wing added on one side in 1845, and the other side in 1869, and further twentieth-century extensions.

The former Salisbury General Infirmary.

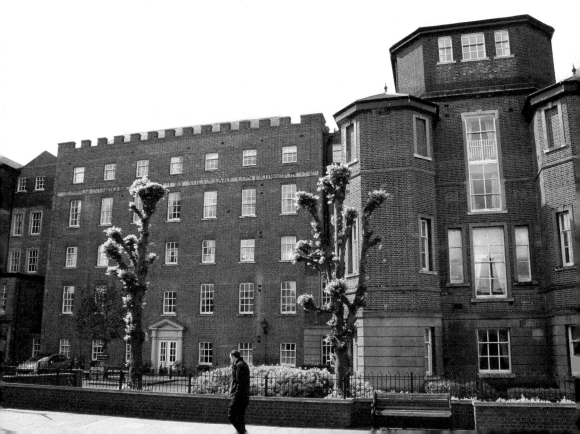

A new outpatients department, dedicated to T. E. Lawrence, the British military officer, was opened in 1936. The hospital joined the National Health Service in 1948. The building was recorded as Grade II listed in 1972 under the name 'General Infirmary'.

It was in the intensive care unit at the infirmary that Phil Lynott, lead singer of Thin Lizzy, died from an alcohol- and drugs-related illness in January 1986. After services transferred to the Salisbury District Hospital in 1991, the infirmary closed in 1993. The building was converted for residential use in 1997.

37. Guildhall and Council House

'The Bishop's Guildhall' dates back to medieval times, but after being demolished because the bishop couldn't afford to maintain it, a new building was erected in 1795 that was designed by Sir Robert Taylor and William Pilkington. To the north of the Bishop's Guildhall stood the Council House, which was the headquarters for the Merchant's Guild, which burnt down 1780. The 2nd Earl of Radnor

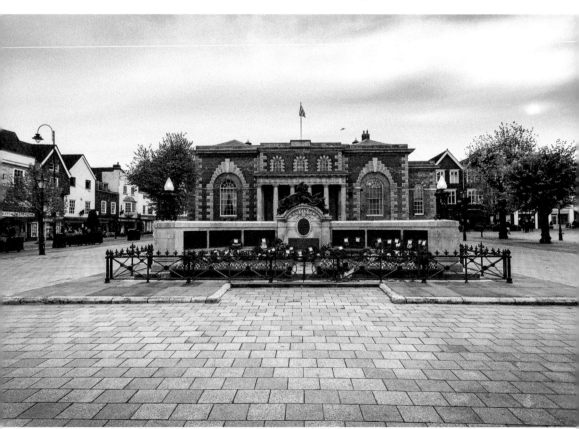

The Guildhall and war memorial.

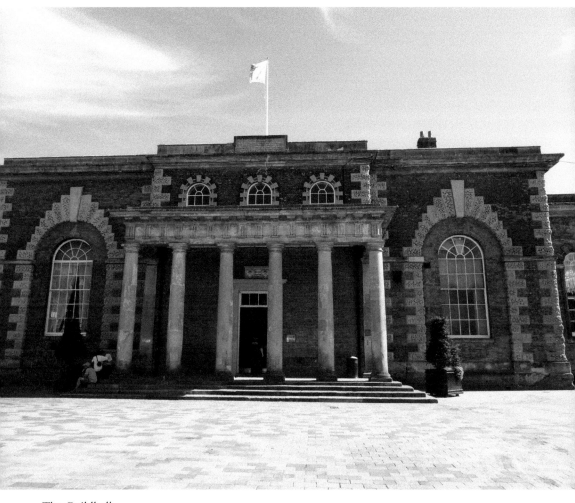

The Guildhall.

paid for the restoration out of his own pocket and work was also started on the Bishop's Guildhall at the same time.

Many alterations have been made since that time including, in 1829, the addition of a Grand Jury Room, rooms for the judges and extensions to the court rooms. The building is now Grade II listed and was described as 'a substantial and handsome building of white brick, ornamented with rustic quoins and cornices of stone'.

In 2011, Salisbury City Council moved its offices into the Guildhall and further refurbishments were undertaken. The current Guildhall is now a popular and impressive wedding, conference and events venue. The names of the rooms reflect the building's legal past, such as the Judge's Retirement Room, Grand Jury Room and Crown Court, which features a beautifully carved mahogany 'Mayor's Chair' over which is an original fitting from 1795 called the 'Judge's Canopy'. This room was the scene of court issues until 2010.

38. Husseys Almshouses

By an indenture dated 1794, William Hussey gave fifteen houses in Castle Street to found an almshouse. Ten of these were to be allotted to the aged and infirm poor, preferably married couples, and these were to be maintained by the rents from the remaining five. In 1809, Hussey also gave the income on an investment of £3,500 to provide weekly pensions for the almspeople. By 1833, the original ten houses had been reconstructed to provide thirteen homes, but the rent from the five houses was insufficient to keep the almshouses in repair. At this time the thirteen almspeople received weekly pensions, which had been increased in 1824 from 2s 10d to 3s 6d, and any deficiency was supplied from Popley's charity. The almshouse was included in the Consolidated Almshouses and Other Charities Scheme of 1871. A further scheme of 1895 provided that the almshouse should accommodate seven married couples, six unmarried persons and a nurse. The almshouse was rebuilt in 1874, and some of the larger houses then contained a workshop.

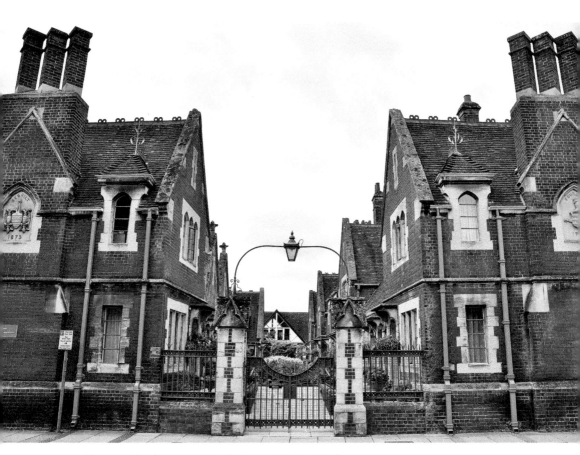

Husseys Almshouses on Castle Street. (© Ben Abel)

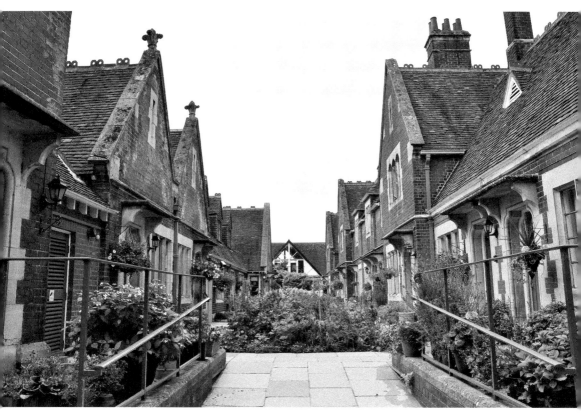

The beautiful external spaces of Husseys Almshouses. (© Ben Abel)

39. St Osmund's Church

It was recorded that there were Roman Catholics in Salisbury before 1672, but the first Jesuit priest, James Weldon, did not arrive in the city until 1765. He was succeeded in 1767 by James Porter, who was chaplain to Raymond Arundell, whose house became a mass centre in Salisbury. By 1780, there was a congregation of forty to fifty people meeting at Arundell's house. After 1792, a chapel was created in the attic of Mary Arundell's house in the square (later St Thomas's Square) and the congregation increased. They also provided shelter for emigrant priests from France. The Catholic Arundell family of Wardour Castle provided moral and financial backing for Roman Catholic churches in the county for around 150 years.

In 1797, the house of Thomas Peniston in Cathedral Close was certified for worship with the Abbe Nicholis Begin but the cathedral chapter objected. Begin then registered a house in Brown Street. In 1814, this was replaced by St Martin's Chapel, partly financed by Lord Arundell, in St Martin's Lane. Begin, who undertook much charitable work among the poor, died in 1826. The first meeting to consider the replacement of St Martin's, which was now too small, took place on 26 October 1846. John Lambert, who was later to become the first Catholic mayor of a cathedral city since the Reformation, was the driving force in the project. A site in Exeter Street owned by congregation member John Peniston was chosen, and the benediction of the foundation stone took place on 8 April 1847. The consecration and opening ceremony took place on 6 and 7 September and the parish was officially established. The church was designed by famous architect A. W. Pugin and much of the cost borne by John Lambert, who had spent his early life at Wardour. In 1851, the average congregation was 170 who lived throughout southern Wiltshire. In an 1865 record of the parish there were 202 people from the parish and 28 from Amesbury, Odstock, Wilton and Barford St Martin. It was estimated that of these 230 there were probably around 25 per cent who were non-Catholic spouses or doubtful practitioners.

The widowed Lady Elizabeth Herbert had been received into the Catholic church at Palermo and, on her return to England, she became patron of the Salisbury mission. She provided the money for a permanent priest and established a parish

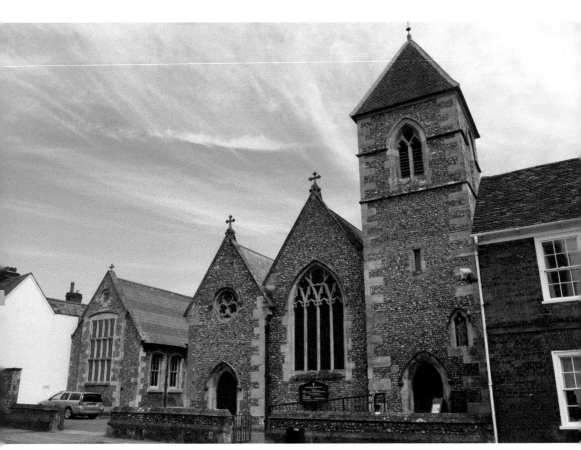

St Osmund's Church.

school beside the church. In the late nineteenth century Salisbury experienced rapid growth in population and St Osmund's became too small for its congregation. In 1894, a north aisle extension was planned and built, and the congregation continued to grow. In 1932, Father Hyland arrived and was to remain at the church for thirty-two years. Although something of an eccentric, he was a figure of authority and influential in the parish, becoming a canon. St Osmund's now covers only the centre and south of the city as there are now three Roman Catholic parishes in the city.

40. Former Market House (Corn Exchange) and Salisbury Library

The former Cheesemarket and Maidenhead Inn was originally run by one Joseph Hibberd, along with his wife Jane, and were present together up until 1827. The inn was eventually replaced by the Market House, eventually known as the Corn Exchange, which was built in 1858 and opened on 24 May 1859. By that year, to assist in maintaining the success of the market, a branch line was opened running from the main station. This lasted until the 1960s. Sadly, the market has gone, along with the branch line, but in its place is a new library, which opened in 1975. In an act of positive conservation, the façade was retained and incorporated into the new library facility.

Designed by the chief engineer of the London & South Western Railway, John Strapp, though much of the original interior of the building has been lost.

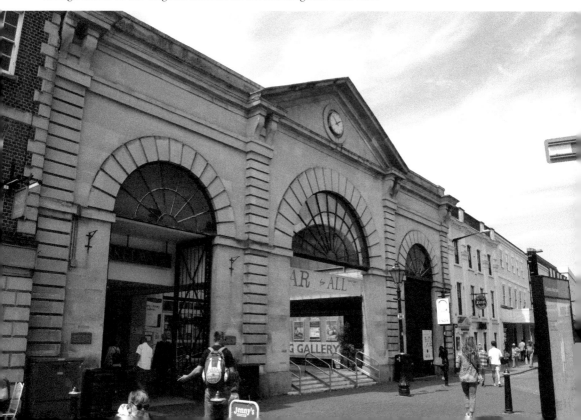

41. Salisbury Railway Station, Fisherton Street

Salisbury was slow to share in Britain's railway mania; it was not until 1847 that a branch line of the London & South Western Railway (LSWR) from Southampton brought rail traffic to the city. This line terminated at Milford on the eastern outskirts of the city. Within ten years a new line had been constructed via Andover, also as part of the LSWR, which terminated at Milford. Between 1856 and 1859, further railway lines arrived in Salisbury. The first of these was laid in 1856 when the Wiltshire, Somerset & Weymouth Railway (an off-shoot of the Great Western Railway) completed a single-track line from Warminster to Salisbury. The line used a broad-gauge track and the trains terminated at a new station in Fisherton, which was designed by the nineteenth-century engineer Isambard Kingdom Brunel. Facilities at the terminus included a four-track layout with two platforms and an all-over roof in typical GWR style, an engine shed and a goods yard. In 1859, a second station was built, just to the south west of the Great Western terminus, by the Salisbury and Yeovil Railway Company; the London and South Western Railway also moved to this new station at Fisherton shortly after. A footbridge was erected to connect the GWR terminus with the adjacent LWSR (later the Southern Railway) station, but this was removed in 1956.

Following the extension of the Yeovil line to Exeter in 1860, and the conversion of the Warminster line from broad gauge to standard gauge in 1874, Salisbury now had the makings of an important railway junction, standing at the crossroads of two significant railway lines.

The railway station on Fisherton Street.

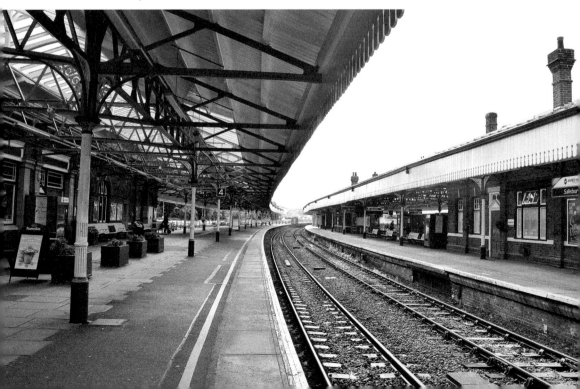

Brunel's terminus was closed to passenger traffic in 1932 when trains of the Southern Railway began using the adjacent former LSWR station. It was then used as a goods station, but since the mid-twentieth century the tracks have been removed and the buildings have alternative uses.

42. School of Arts Annexe

This Grade I listed building in New Street was originally an art gallery provided by Dr Roberts and formed part of Hamilton Hall, built in 1871 as the Literary and Scientific Institute. Salisbury Corporation took it over in 1894. It became the City of Salisbury School of Art in 1927, delivering fine and applied arts courses. There was name change in 1935 when it became known as the City of Salisbury School of Art & Crafts, and additional subject areas were added including drawing, painting, modelling, architecture and design (industrial and pictorial).

The School of Arts moved to a new site as Salisbury College of Art and Design in the 1960s and merged with Salisbury College of Technology in 1992, staying on the same site eventually becoming Salisbury College, forming part of Wiltshire College.

The School of Arts Annexe.

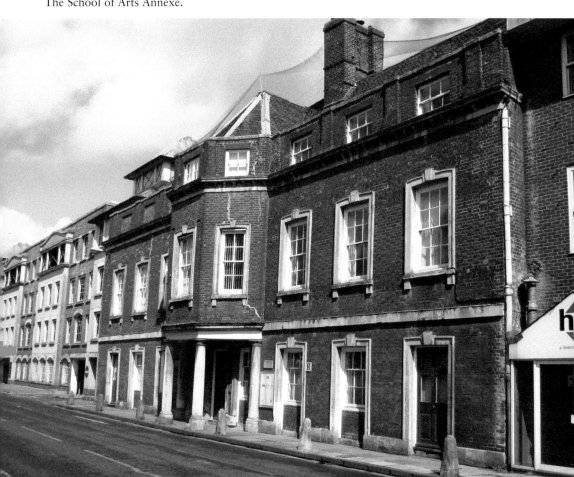

43. The Former County Hotel, now The King's Head

The King's Head Inn in Bridge Street has been an inn since the fourteenth century and has been known as The Lion Inn, The Ramme, The King's Head and the King's Head and Brewery. In 1874, it was rebuilt for the Richardson brothers, who were wine and spirit importers, shippers and wholesalers, and who were then Britain's oldest wine and spirit business, eventually becoming known as the County Hotel. It was used as a wine merchants up to the twentieth century.

The King's Head is mentioned in a book by John Taylor, known as 'the water poet', which was published at the end of Queen Elizabeth's reign. The following was written about his boat journey with five others from Christchurch on the River Avon.

> At tymes ... 2,000 swans, like pilots, going before us to show us the way. At Fordingbridge an unfortunate misadventure befell. For two men being swimming or washing in the river, a butcher passing over the bridge (with a mastiff dog with him) did cast a stone into the water, and say, A duck; at which, the dog leaped into the river, and seized upon one of the men and killed him; and the butcher leaping in after, thinking to save the man, was also slain by his own dog, the third man also hardly escaping, but was likewise bitten by him.

The inn was refurbished by the national pub and restaurant chain, Wetherspoon's, and reopened in 2002 and reverted back to being known as The King's Head.

The former County Hotel, now The King's Head Inn.

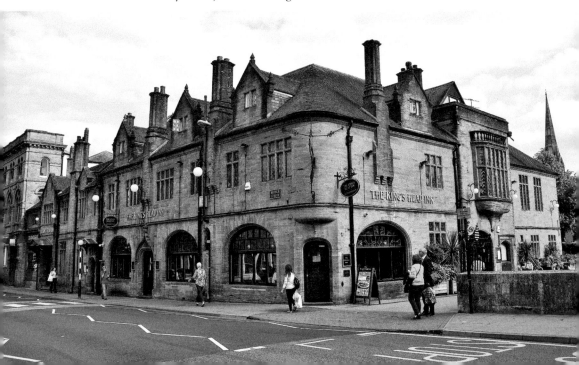

44. Maundrell Hall

The hall was opened in 1880 alongside Fisherton Bridge and named after one of Fisherton's Protestant martyrs. John Maundrell was one of three men burnt on 23 March 1556 at 'a place between Salisbury and Wilton'. Legend says that the place of execution was on the site of the gallows, just to the west of the present Church of St Paul.

The hall was provided by public subscription and was intended as a place for undenominational worship and discussion, especially for poor people who were not regular churchgoers. Other buildings were erected on the site, including a temperance hotel (1883) and the Princess Christian Home (later Hostel) for Women.

After the building of a new Parochial Hall in 1937 and a westward shift in population, the Maundrell Hall lost much of its usefulness. With adjoining buildings, it was sold in 1954. It is now a public house.

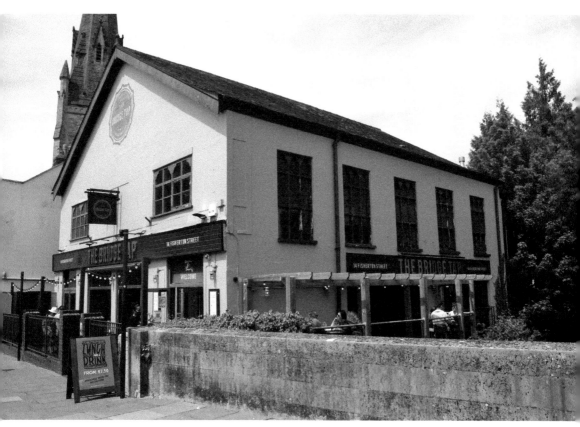

Maundrell Hall, now a public house. John Maundrell, William and Alice Moberley, and John Spicer were all burned together at two stakes in March 1556 for holding Protestant beliefs during the reign of Queen Mary. It was recorded that they 'most constantly gave their bodies to the fire, and their souls to the Lord for the testimony of His truth'. Three wandering minstrels were also burned to death for their beliefs.

45. Clock Tower, Fisherton Street

The Grade II listed Clock Tower on Fisherton Street is nicknamed by locals as 'Little Ben' and the clock is illuminated with four dials. Dating back to 1892, it was built by Dr John Roberts as a memorial for his wife, Arabella.

A fascinating locally known fact is that the base of the tower formed part of one of the three gaols in Salisbury, and dates from 1631 with a number of Georgian alterations. There is a plaque on the west wall that has a carving of three leg

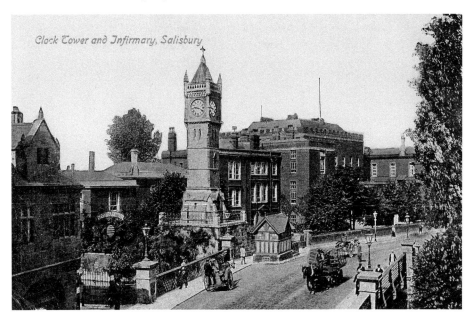

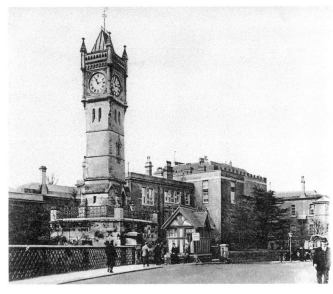

Above: The clock tower on Fisherton Street and Infirmary.

Left: The Clock Tower, known as Little Ben.

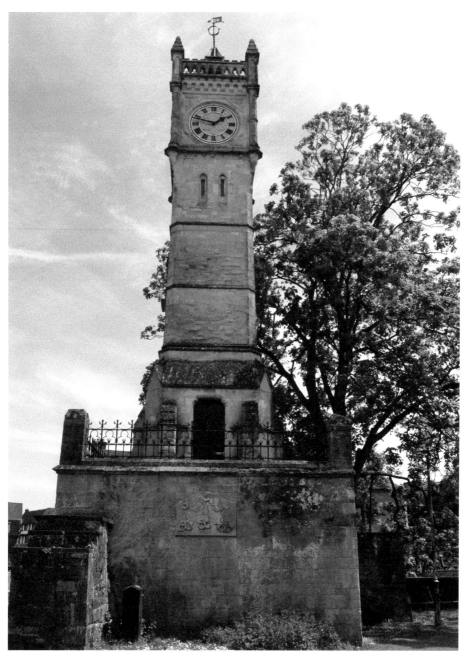

The clock tower on Fisherton Street.

irons with chains that give testament to the history of the site. Although the main gaol was sold to the neighbouring infirmary in 1822 and then demolished, the tower was added and the cells beneath it were used for many years where local drunks were given a bed for the night.

46. New Sarum House, Blue Boar Row

Blue Boar Row faces the Market Place and its unusual name comes from an inn that once stood on the site from at least the fifteenth century, and certainly up into the nineteenth century.

The Grade II listed New Sarum House on Blue Boar Row is one of the finest buildings in this locality. It was originally commercial chambers built in 1900 by

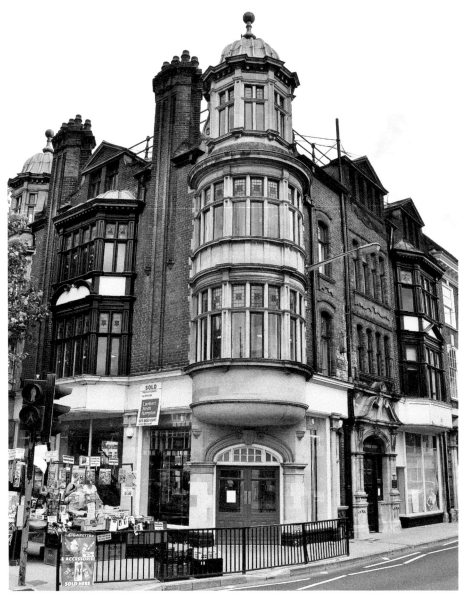

The Grade II listed New Sarum House on Blue Boar Row.

Frederick Bath of Salisbury. Built of red brick, ashlar and timber bay windows, it has a clay, plain tile roof with railings around lead flats and is very much in the Jacobean/Dutch style.

17. The Church of St Francis of Assisi

The church was founded in 1930 to serve the north of the city. Work began in 1930, with the consent of the vicars of Stratford-sub-Castle and St Marks's. With much voluntary help a temporary wooden church was built on the eastern side of Stratford Road and dedicated in November 1930. In 1937, a new district was established, partly from the parish of Stratford-sub-Castle and partly from that of St Mark's, and a vicar was installed. In the same year, a building committee was formed and a new site at the junction of Beatrice Road and Castle Road purchased. Building work began in 1938, the foundation stone was laid in January 1939 and the church was consecrated in 1940.

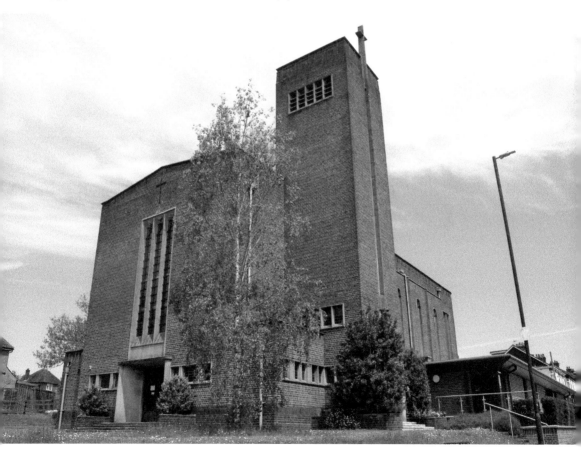

The Church of St Francis of Assisi.

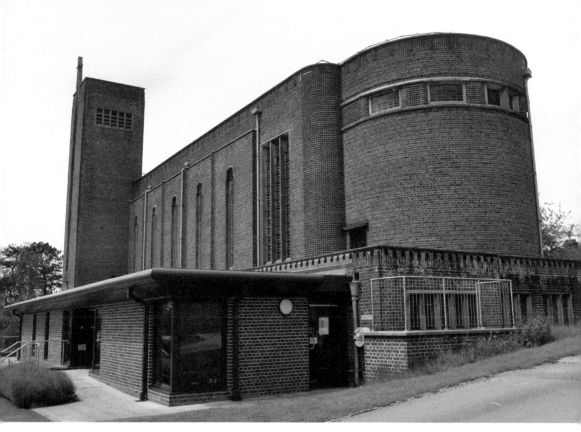

The church acquired the bells of the church of St Giles at Imber, which no longer had need of them.

The church building is in a twentieth-century style with a wide nave, with passage aisles and an apsidal Lady Chapel behind the sanctuary instead of a chancel. On the south side of the church is a tower that is 70 feet (21 metres) high. The building was designed by the architect Robert Potter. It is structurally concrete with brick cladding and infill, and the church has artificial stone surrounds to the doors and windows. The cavity walls are faced with variegated red bricks and the dressings are of reconstituted stone. The roofs are of reinforced concrete covered with asphalt. The church is now Grade II listed.

The Wiltshire volume of Nikolaus Pevsner's *Buildings of England* includes a short entry on the church: 'St Francis, Castle Road and Beatrice Road. 1936–9 by Robert Potter. Red brick. Square, with a short s w tower and an apse. The details Österbergish – rather late in the day. Quite an impressive white interior, the floor of the apse raised considerably above the altar space.'

In the twenty-first century the church has had a £450,000 renovation to bring the building up to modern standards. One-tenth of the renovation funds raised (£45,000) were given away to build a secondary school in Juba in South Sudan.

48. Salisbury Law Courts

This imposing new building, completed in 2009, is the first combined court centre in the country and is a groundbreaker for Her Majesty's Court Service. Feilden+Mawson architects were appointed in 2002 to act as lead designers and technical advisors for the new courthouse, which comprises two crown and two magistrates' courts, a district judge's hearing room and the regional office. It is located in the Salisbury City Conservation Area. The design and choice of materials draw from the local semi-urban townscape and palette to achieve a civic presence, which was intended to spark regeneration on a main route into the city.

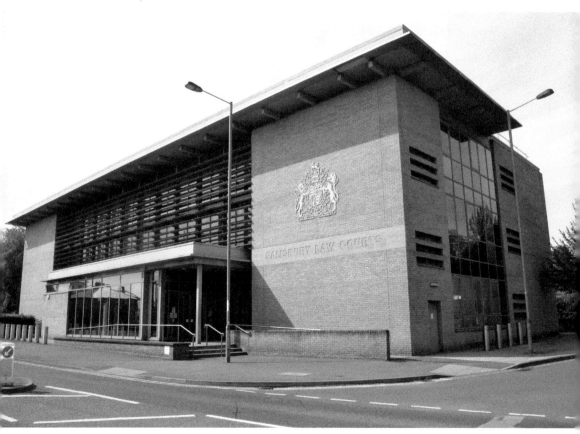

The modern Salisbury Law Courts.

49. Nos 1 and 3 Castle Street (currently Zizzi's)

No story about Salisbury could be told without mention of the shocking events that took place on 4 March 2018 when Sergei Skripal, a former Russian military officer and double agent for the UK's intelligence services, and his daughter Yulia Skripal were poisoned. The couple had eaten at Zizzi's Italian restaurant in Castle Street before falling unconscious on a bench outside.

Traces of the novichok nerve agent were found in the restaurant, which was immediately sealed off and closed down for a deep clean before reopening in November 2018. Sergei and Yulia remained in critical condition for three weeks before both making a full recovery. Russia was accused by the British government of attempted murder, who then began an expulsion of Russian diplomats who were resident in the country. Russia retaliated by accusing Britain of the poisoning and also began a series of expulsions.

In June 2018, there was a similar poisoning with novichok in Amesbury, which is 7 miles north of Salisbury. It was found in a perfume bottle that was sprayed onto the wrist of a local women, Dawn Sturgess, who immediately fell ill and sadly died. It is not believed that the poisoning was connected, but rather how the nerve agent was disposed of following the first poisoning.

The city's tourist industry was badly hit after the poisonings as the city centre was effectively sealed off for forensic testing, investigation and cleaning.

The fenced-off and secure Zizzi's on Market Place after the notorious attack here in 2018.

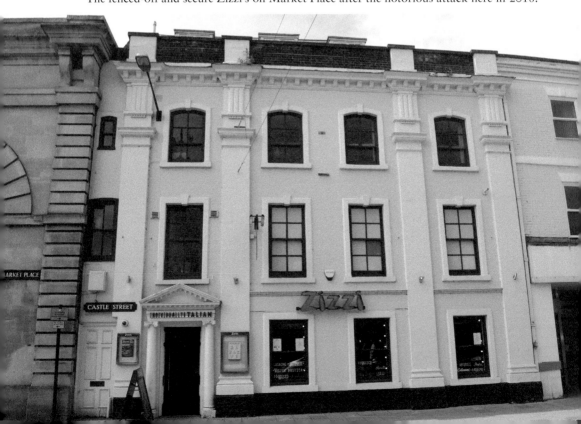

Visitor numbers considerably decreased, with the cathedral in particular reporting numbers down to 29 per cent of the same period the previous year. However, its heart is beating strongly again, and this historic centre continues to flourish.

50. Salisbury District Council Offices Extension

Stanton Williams architects were commissioned to design new offices for Wiltshire Council on a sensitive historic site at Bourne Hill. The new council building is a marriage of a new building and the restored Grade II* listed Bourne Hill House. The new building has 2,600 square metres of flexible, open-plan offices that enjoy generous views of the surrounding gardens. Externally, it is given presence and scale by a full-height colonnade set in front of its glazed elevations, and there is thus a strong relationship between the architecture and the external landscape. The design incorporates an integral low-energy strategy in order to achieve an 'excellent' energy rating.

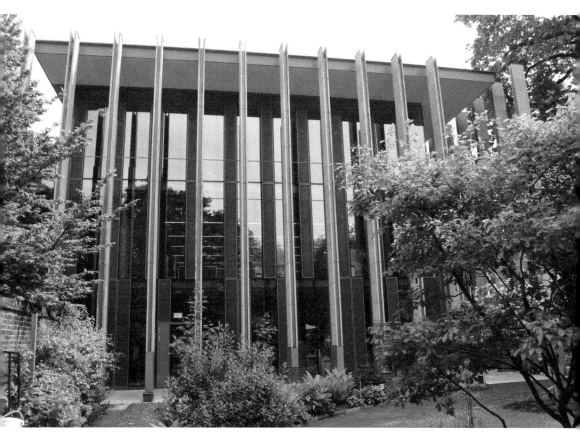

A modern extension to the current council offices.

Bourne Hill House has been fully restored. It had been subjected to a series of detrimental external additions and these accretions have been swept away, reinforcing the architectural integrity of the house. On a sensitive site and within an historic city, the final design was arrived at following an extensive process of consultation with the local community and with expert bodies, including English Heritage.

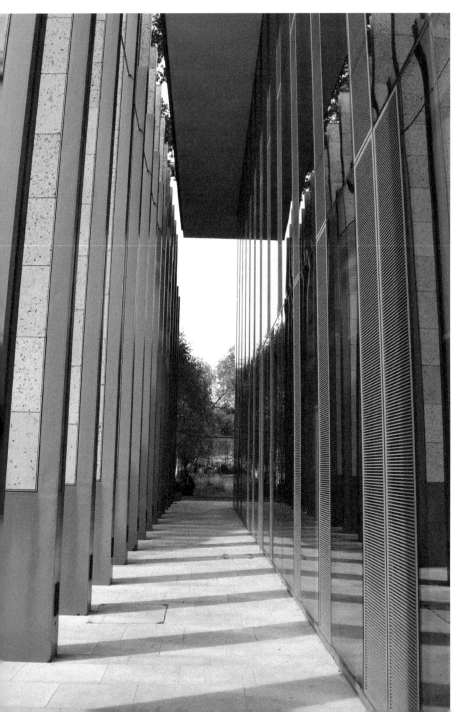

Modern and vibrant in this ancient city.

Bibliography

Websites

archaeology-travel.com
arundells.org
british-history.ac.uk
collegeofmatrons.org.uk
countrylife.co.uk
gatehouse-gazetteer.info
godolphin.org
haunchpub.co.uk
history.wiltshire.gov.uk
milfordstreetbridgeproject.org.uk
nationaltrust.org.uk
salisburyclosepreservation.org
salisburymethodist.org.uk
salisburyguildhall.co.uk
sarum.ac.uk
stthomassalisbury.co.uk
theguardian.com
the-redlion.co.uk
visitwiltshire.co.uk

Books

Biddle, G. and O. S. Nock, *The Railway Heritage of Britain* (Studio Edition: London, 1983)
Burnett, David., *Salisbury: The History of an English Cathedral City* (Compton Press)
Chandler, J., *Endless Street: A History of Salisbury and Its People* (Hobnob Press: 1983)
Chandler, J., *Salisbury History Around Us* (Hobnob Press, 2004)
Chandler, J., *Salisbury: History and Guide* (Alan Sutton Publishing: Stroud, 1992)

Dixon-Smith, Carol and Catherine Essenhigh, *Salisbury Through Time* (Amberley Publishing: Stroud, 2016)

Garman, Edwin M., *The Public Houses and Inns of Salisbury* (Hobnob Press: 2017)

Hilliam, David., *A Salisbury Miscellany* (The History Press: Stroud, 2013)

Morriss, Richard K. and Ken Hoverd, *The Buildings of Salisbury* (Alan Sutton Publishing: Stroud, 1994)

Newman, Ruth and Jane Howells, *Salisbury Past* (Phillimore: Chichester, 2001)

Purvis, Bruce, *Salisbury: The Changing City* (Breedon Books, 2003)

Saunders, Peter, *Salisbury in Old Photographs* (Alan Sutton Publishing: Gloucester, 1987)

Shortt, Hugh, *City of Salisbury* (Phoenix House Ltd: London, 1957)

Shortt, Hugh, *Salisbury: A New Approach to the City and Its Neighbourhood* (Longman: London, 1972)